W9-BCO-956

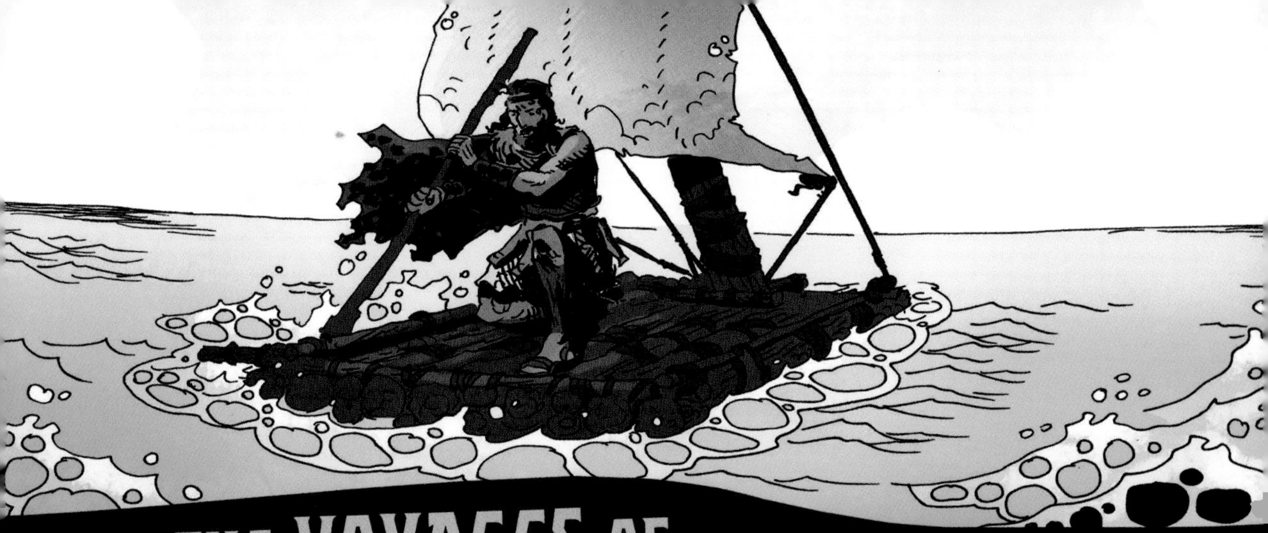

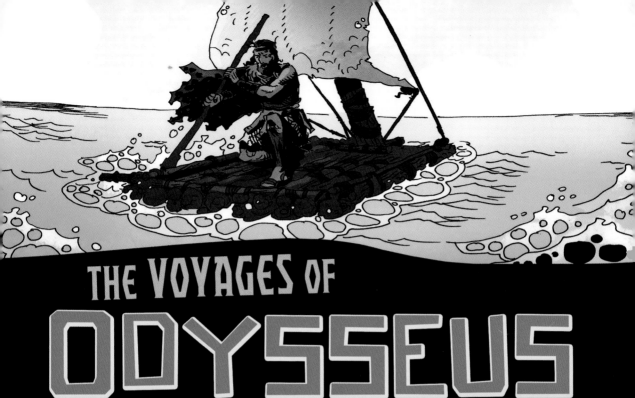

THE VOYAGES OF ODYSSEUS

A GRAPHIC RETELLING

BY BLAKE HOENA

ILLUSTRATED BY ESTUDIO HAUS

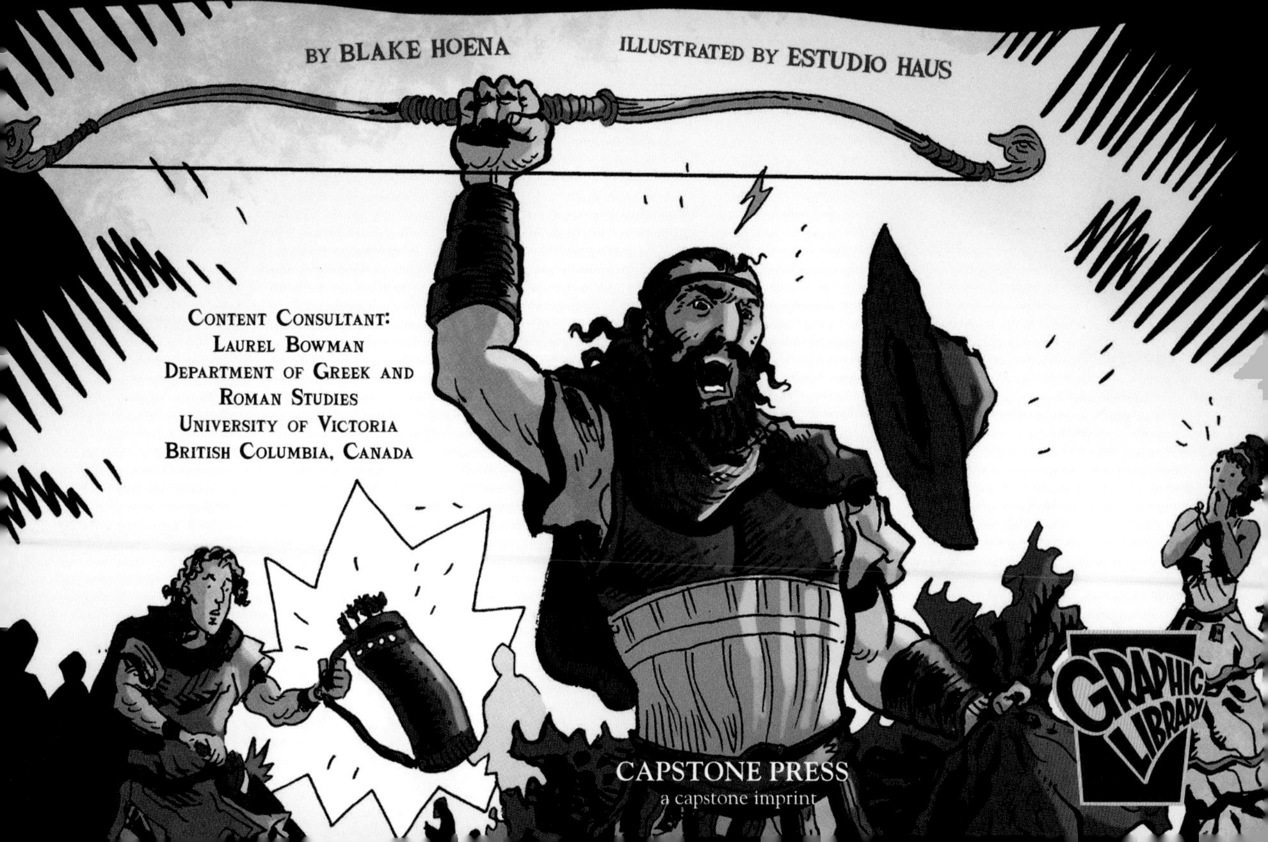

CONTENT CONSULTANT:
LAUREL BOWMAN
DEPARTMENT OF GREEK AND
ROMAN STUDIES
UNIVERSITY OF VICTORIA
BRITISH COLUMBIA, CANADA

GRAPHIC LIBRARY

CAPSTONE PRESS
a capstone imprint

Graphic Library is published by Capstone Press,
1710 Roe Crest Drive, North Mankato, Minnesota 56003
www.capstonepub.com

Library of Congress Cataloging-in-Publication Data
Hoena, B. A., author.
The voyages of Odysseus : a graphic retelling / by Blake Hoena ; illustrated by Estudio Haus.
pages cm.—(Graphic library. Ancient myths)
Summary: "The story of Odysseus' journey told in graphic novel format"—Provided by publisher.
Audience: Ages 8-14.
Audience: Grades 4 to 6.
Includes bibliographical references and index.
ISBN 978-1-4914-2076-8 (library binding)
ISBN 978-1-4914-2280-9 (paperback)
ISBN 978-1-4914-2294-6 (ebook pdf)
1. Odysseus (Greek mythology)—Comic books, strips, etc. 2. Odysseus (Greek mythology)—Juvenile literature. 3. Mythology, Greek—Comic books, strips, etc. 4. Mythology, Greek—Juvenile literature. I. Estudio Haus (Firm), illustrator. II. Title.
BL820.O3H66 2015
398.2'0938—dc23 2014019195

Editor
Anthony Wacholtz

Designer
Ashlee Suker

Art Director
Nathan Gassman

Production Specialist
Tori Abraham

Printed in the United States of America in Stevens Point, Wisconsin
092014 008479WZS15

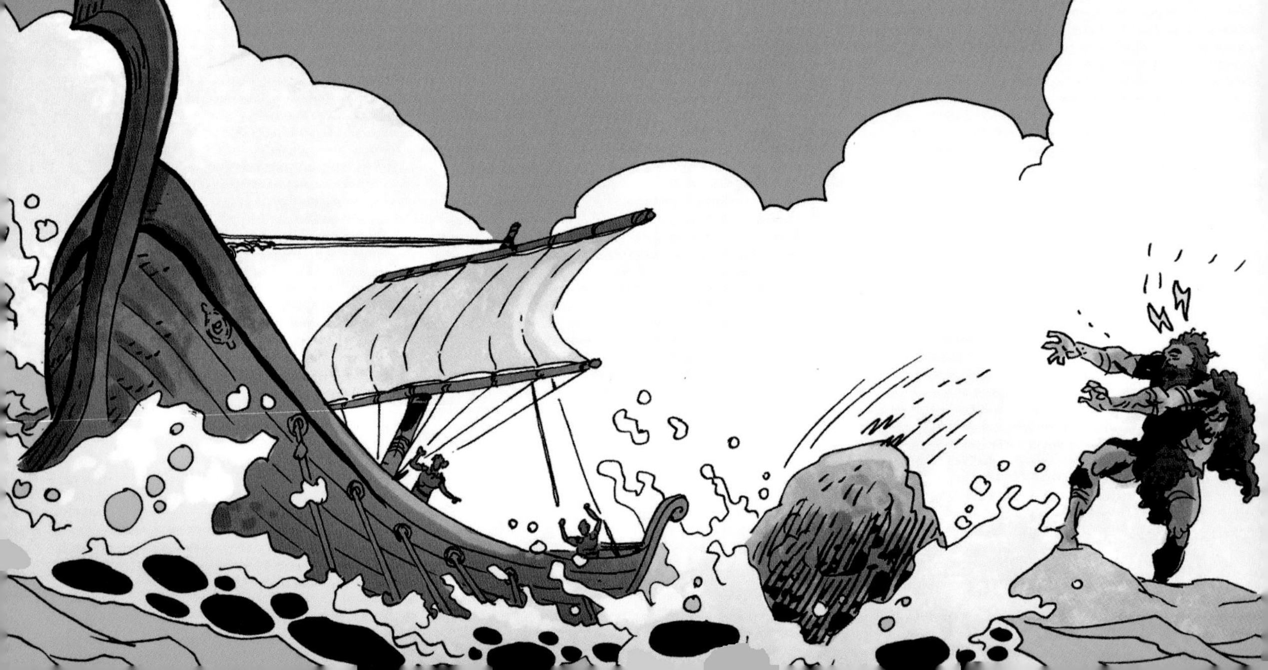

TABLE OF CONTENTS

ORIGINS OF THE MYTH

The Greek poet Homer (8th century BC) composed two books, *The Iliad* and *The Odyssey*, that retell epic tales from ancient times. While *The Iliad* describes the Trojan War, *The Odyssey* follows Odysseus' troubled journey home after the war's end. This retelling of Odysseus' travels is based on Homer's work.

CHAPTER ONE

TROUBLE WITH THE GODS

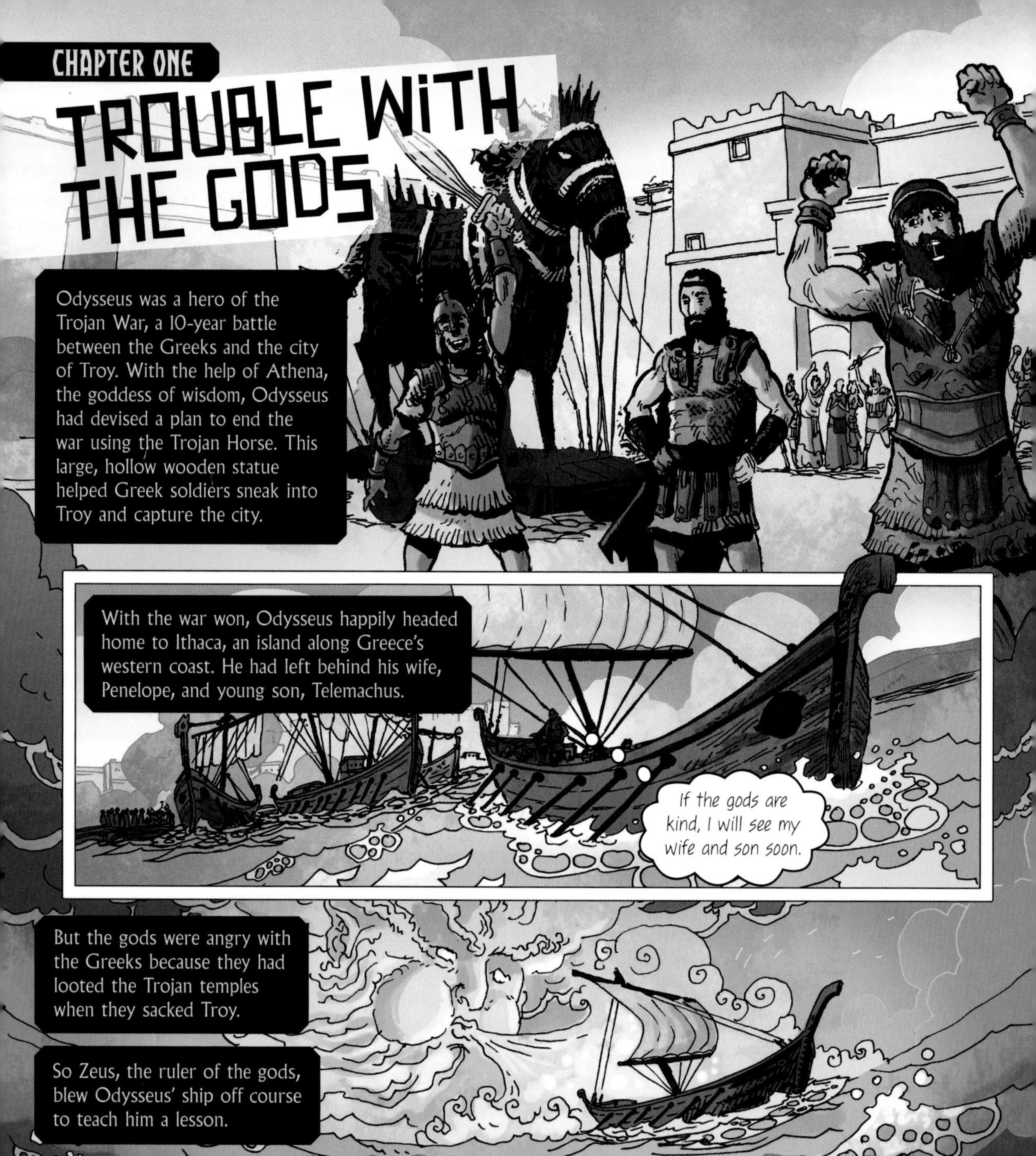

Odysseus was a hero of the Trojan War, a 10-year battle between the Greeks and the city of Troy. With the help of Athena, the goddess of wisdom, Odysseus had devised a plan to end the war using the Trojan Horse. This large, hollow wooden statue helped Greek soldiers sneak into Troy and capture the city.
With the war won, Odysseus happily headed home to Ithaca, an island along Greece's western coast. He had left behind his wife, Penelope, and young son, Telemachus.
If the gods are kind, I will see my wife and son soon.
But the gods were angry with the Greeks because they had looted the Trojan temples when they sacked Troy.
So Zeus, the ruler of the gods, blew Odysseus' ship off course to teach him a lesson.

ANCIENT FACT

The Trojan War began when Prince Paris of Troy stole Helen from her husband Menelaus. Helen was considered the most beautiful woman in the world. Menelaus gathered a large Greek army to take back his wife. But the walls of Troy were tall and strong. The Greeks could not get into the city until soldiers snuck inside while hidden inside the Trojan Horse.

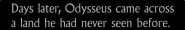

Days later, Odysseus came across a land he had never seen before.

Go find the people that live here. See if they can help us find our way home.

Odysseus eventually went in search of the missing men. He found them just lying about with the natives.

But the men never returned.

The natives had fed the men lotus flowers. People who ate the sweet and delicious flowers completely forgot about all of their cares.

Odysseus' men even forgot about their desire to return home after the 10-year war.

Please, let me stay ...

Drag them back to the ship and we'll set sail. I don't want to risk having anyone else tasting that flower.

But I like it here ...

Just one more taste ...

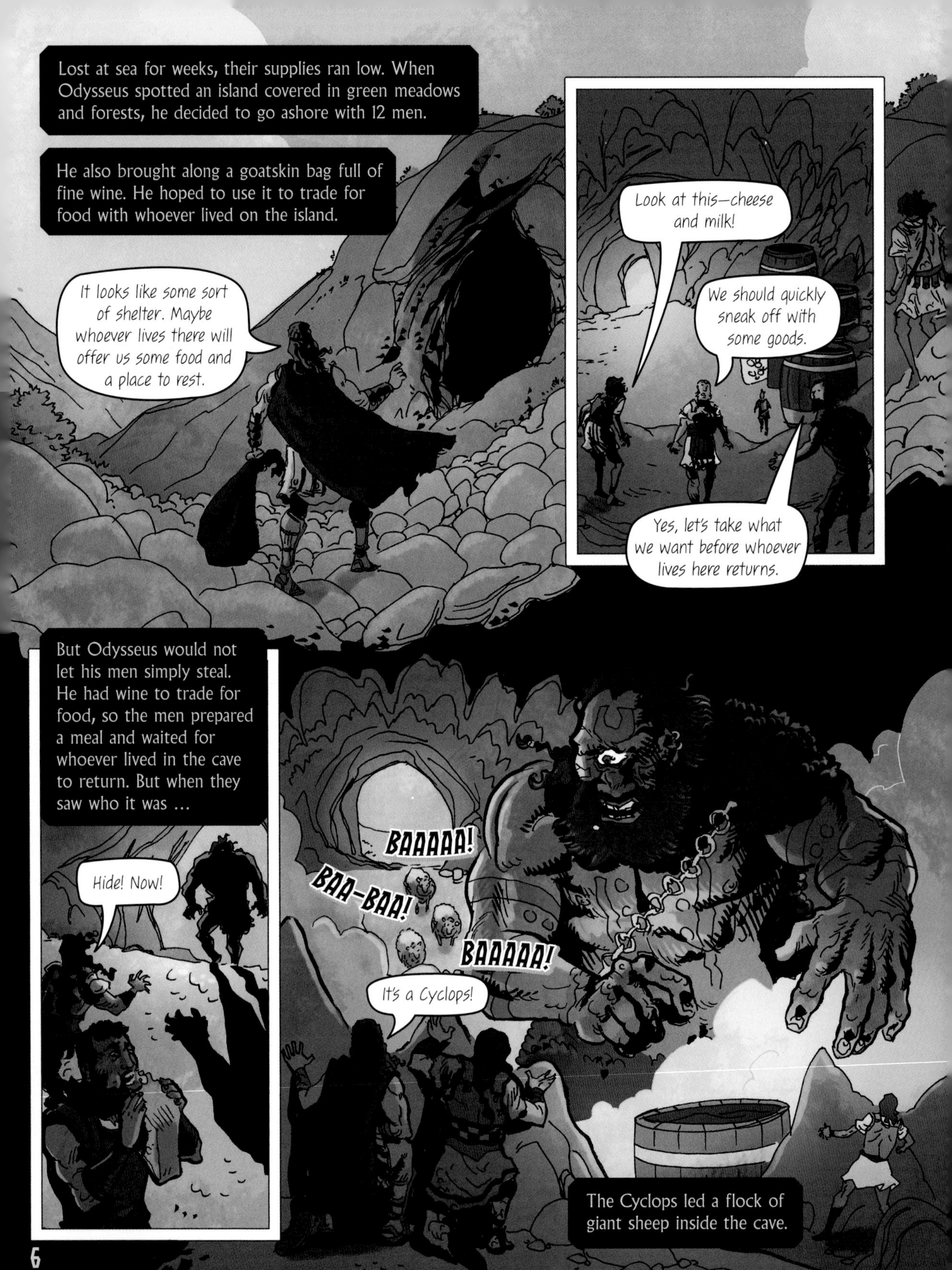

Lost at sea for weeks, their supplies ran low. When Odysseus spotted an island covered in green meadows and forests, he decided to go ashore with 12 men.
He also brought along a goatskin bag full of fine wine. He hoped to use it to trade for food with whoever lived on the island.
It looks like some sort of shelter. Maybe whoever lives there will offer us some food and a place to rest.
Look at this—cheese and milk!
We should quickly sneak off with some goods.
Yes, let's take what we want before whoever lives here returns.
But Odysseus would not let his men simply steal. He had wine to trade for food, so the men prepared a meal and waited for whoever lived in the cave to return. But when they saw who it was …
Hide! Now!
BAAAAA!
BAA-BAA!
BAAAAA!
It's a Cyclops!
The Cyclops led a flock of giant sheep inside the cave.

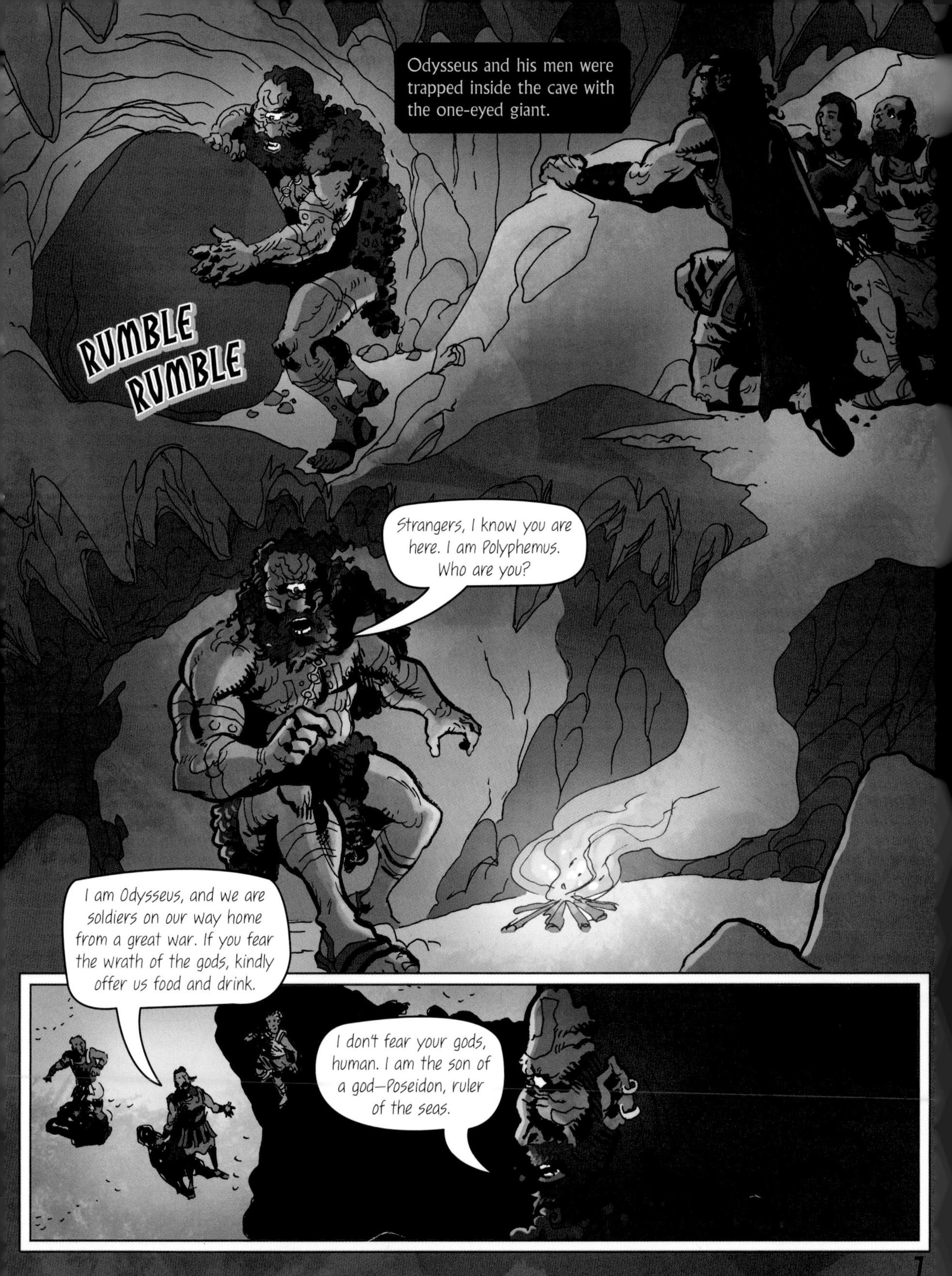
Odysseus and his men were trapped inside the cave with the one-eyed giant.
RUMBLE RUMBLE
Strangers, I know you are here. I am Polyphemus. Who are you?
I am Odysseus, and we are soldiers on our way home from a great war. If you fear the wrath of the gods, kindly offer us food and drink.
I don't fear your gods, human. I am the son of a god—Poseidon, ruler of the seas.

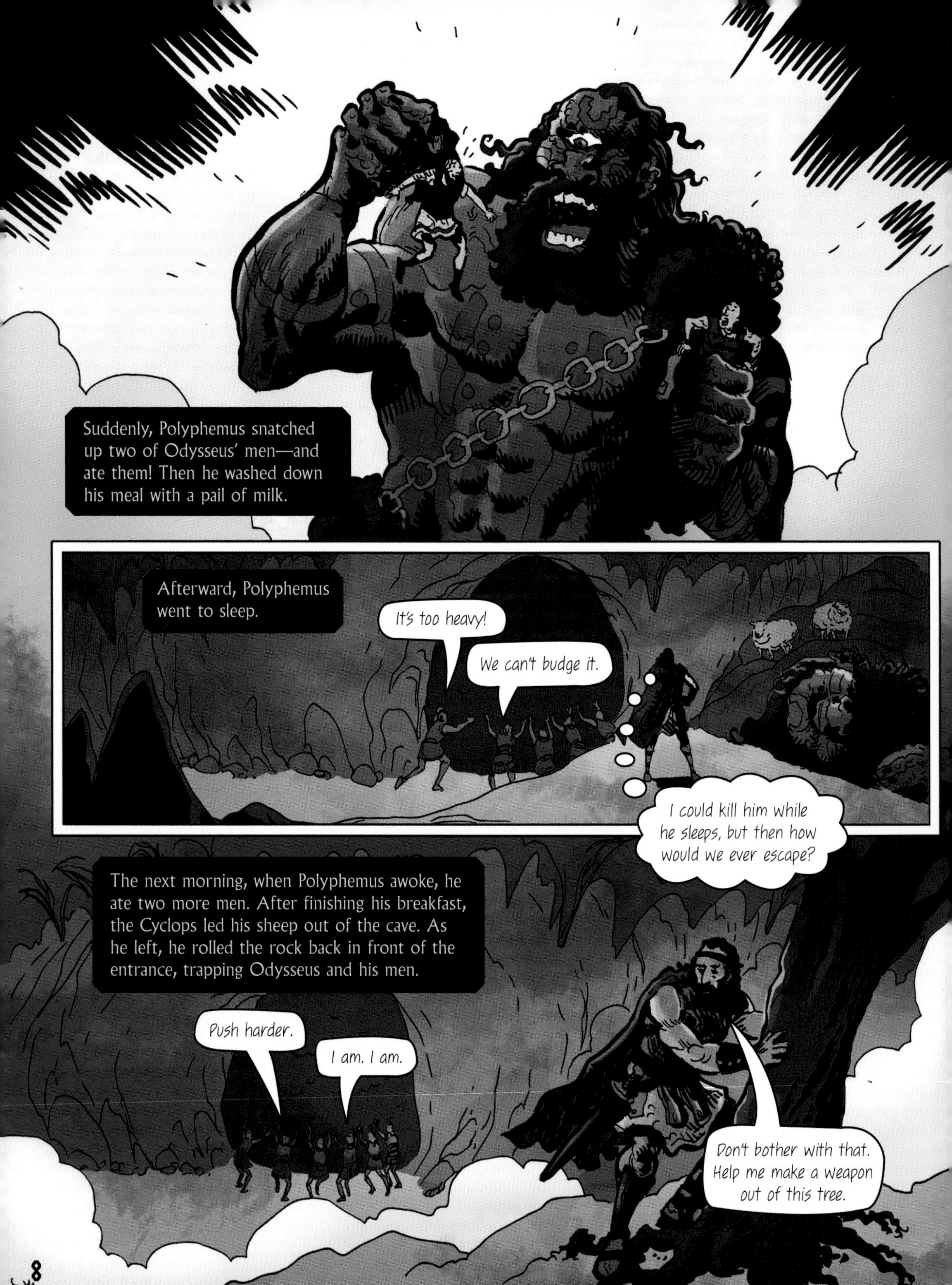

Suddenly, Polyphemus snatched up two of Odysseus' men—and ate them! Then he washed down his meal with a pail of milk.
Afterward, Polyphemus went to sleep.
It's too heavy!
We can't budge it.
I could kill him while he sleeps, but then how would we ever escape?
The next morning, when Polyphemus awoke, he ate two more men. After finishing his breakfast, the Cyclops led his sheep out of the cave. As he left, he rolled the rock back in front of the entrance, trapping Odysseus and his men.
Push harder.
I am. I am.
Don't bother with that. Help me make a weapon out of this tree.

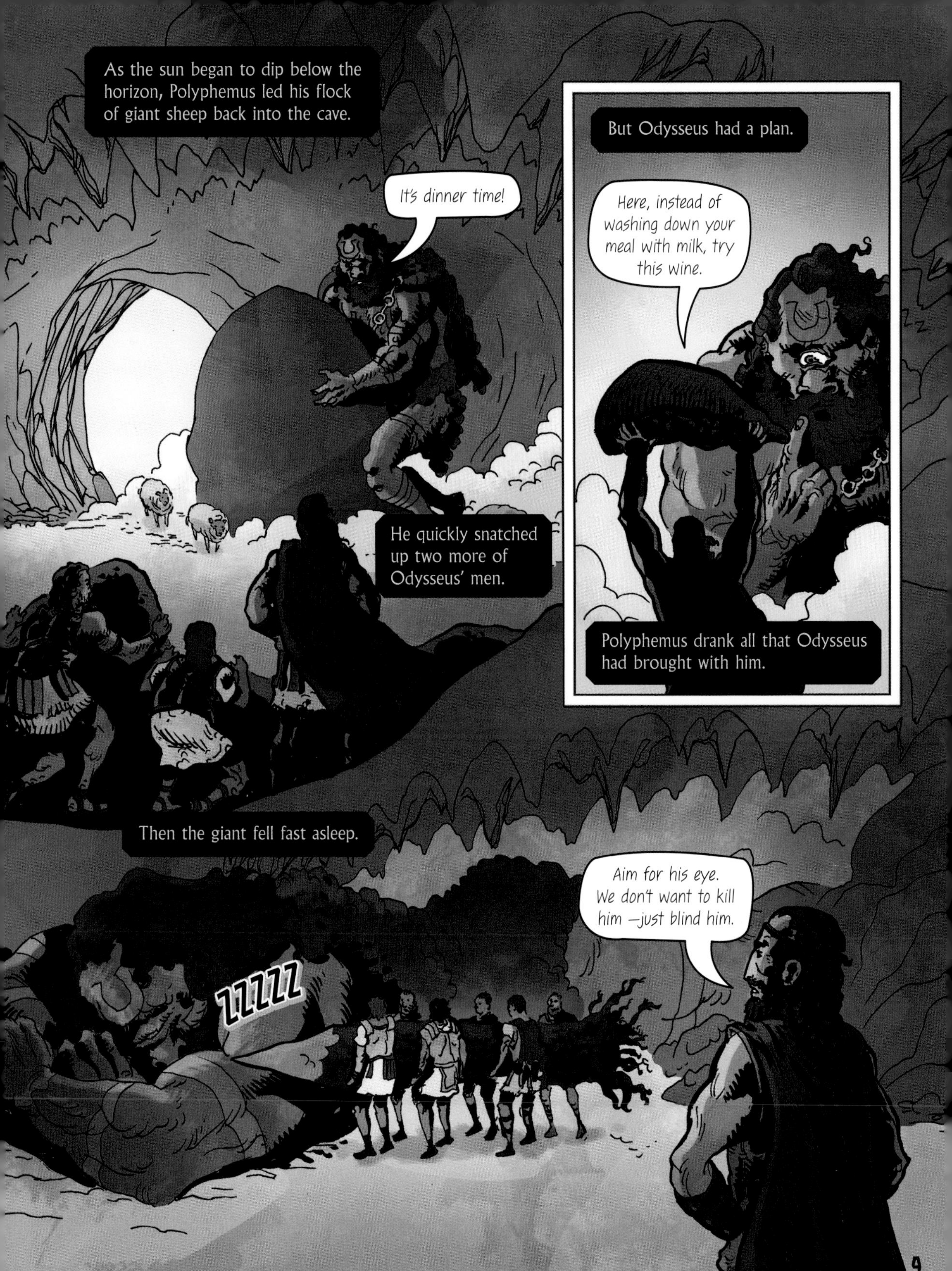
As the sun began to dip below the horizon, Polyphemus led his flock of giant sheep back into the cave.
It's dinner time!
He quickly snatched up two more of Odysseus' men.
But Odysseus had a plan.
Here, instead of washing down your meal with milk, try this wine.
Polyphemus drank all that Odysseus had brought with him.
Then the giant fell fast asleep.
ZZZZZ
Aim for his eye. We don't want to kill him —just blind him.

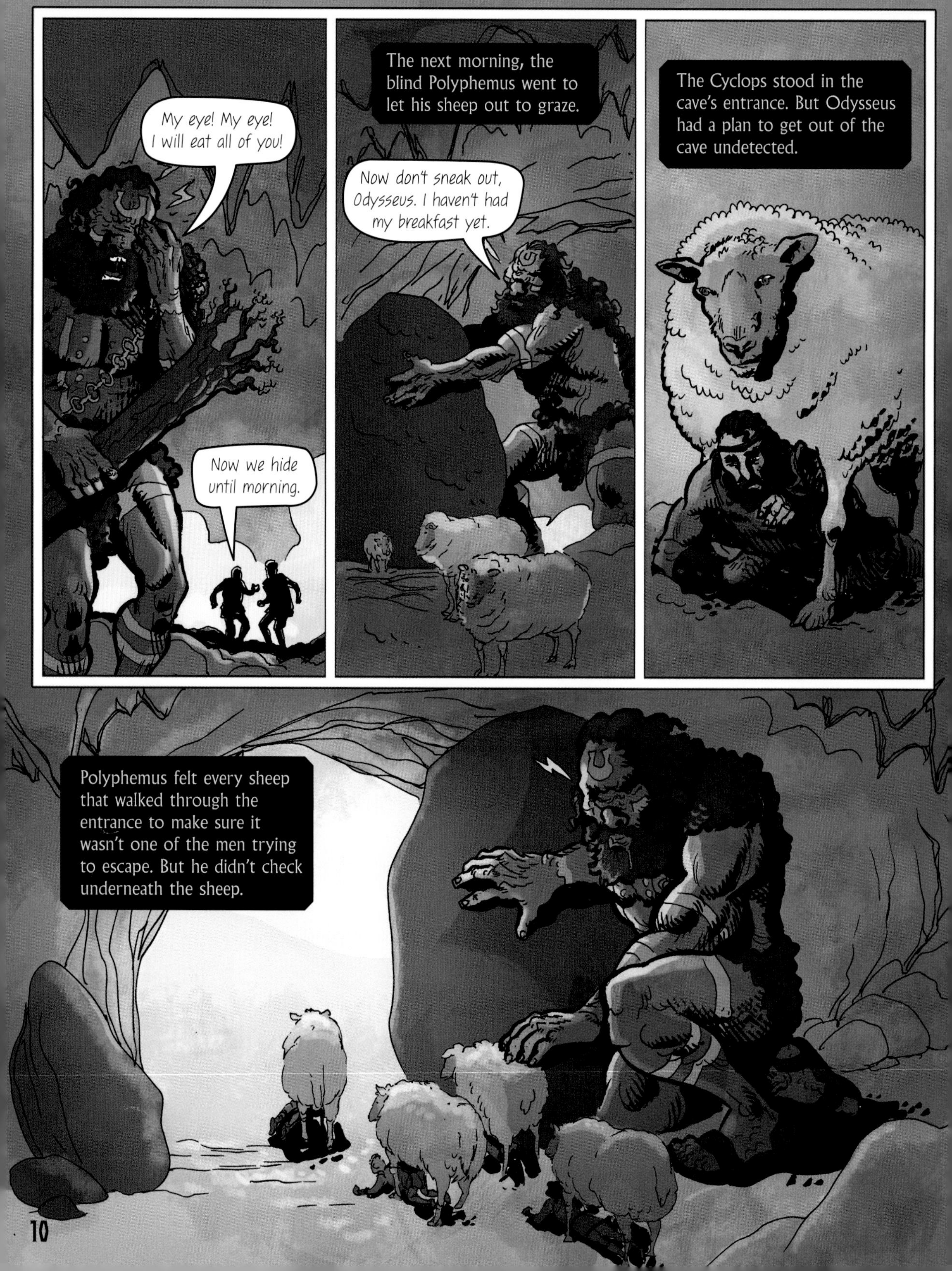
My eye! My eye! I will eat all of you!
Now we hide until morning.
The next morning, the blind Polyphemus went to let his sheep out to graze.
Now don't sneak out, Odysseus. I haven't had my breakfast yet.
The Cyclops stood in the cave's entrance. But Odysseus had a plan to get out of the cave undetected.
Polyphemus felt every sheep that walked through the entrance to make sure it wasn't one of the men trying to escape. But he didn't check underneath the sheep.

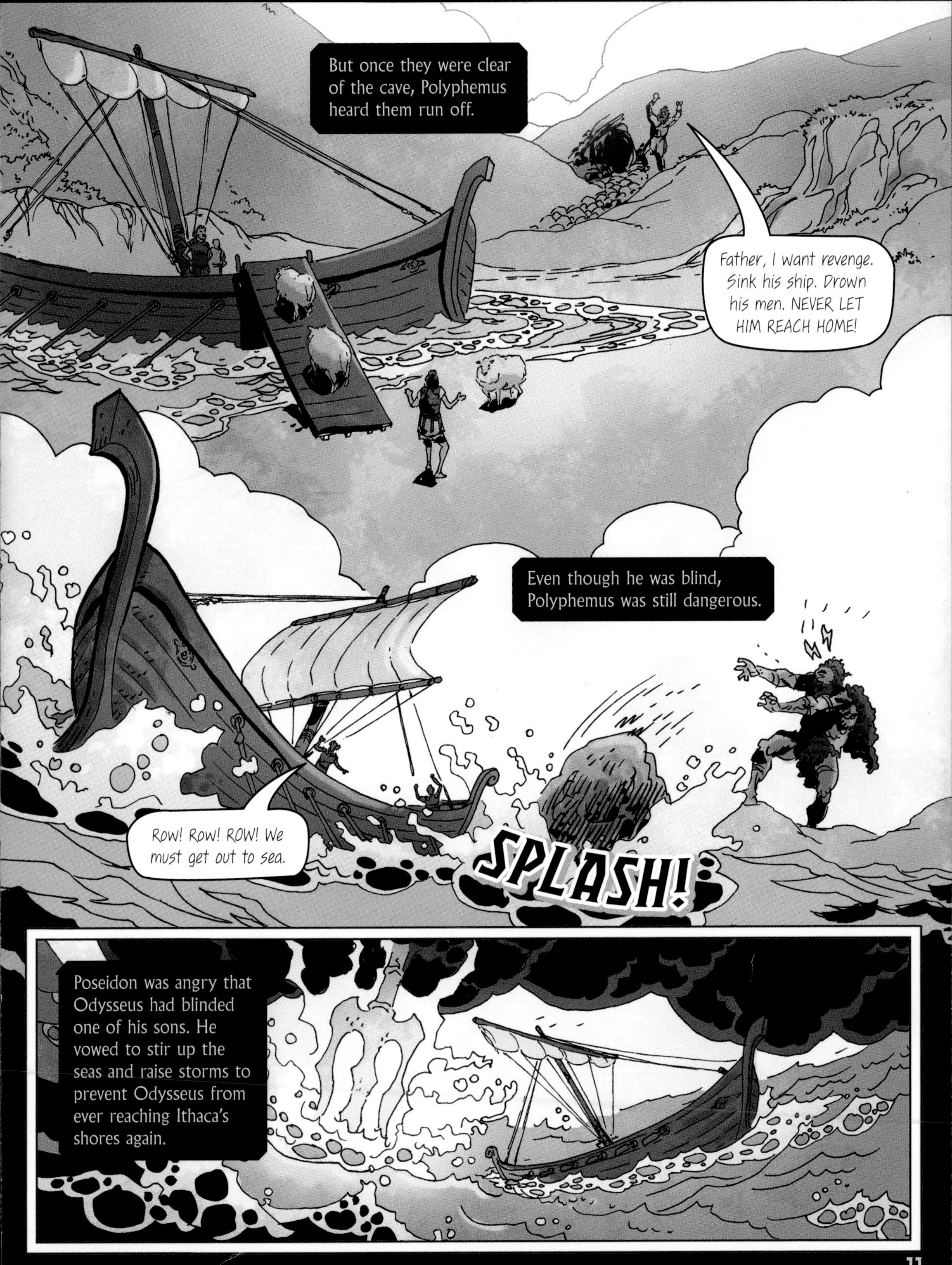

But once they were clear of the cave, Polyphemus heard them run off.
Father, I want revenge. Sink his ship. Drown his men. NEVER LET HIM REACH HOME!
Even though he was blind, Polyphemus was still dangerous.
Row! Row! ROW! We must get out to sea.
SPLASH!
Poseidon was angry that Odysseus had blinded one of his sons. He vowed to stir up the seas and raise storms to prevent Odysseus from ever reaching Ithaca's shores again.

CHAPTER TWO

CIRCE AND THE UNDERWORLD

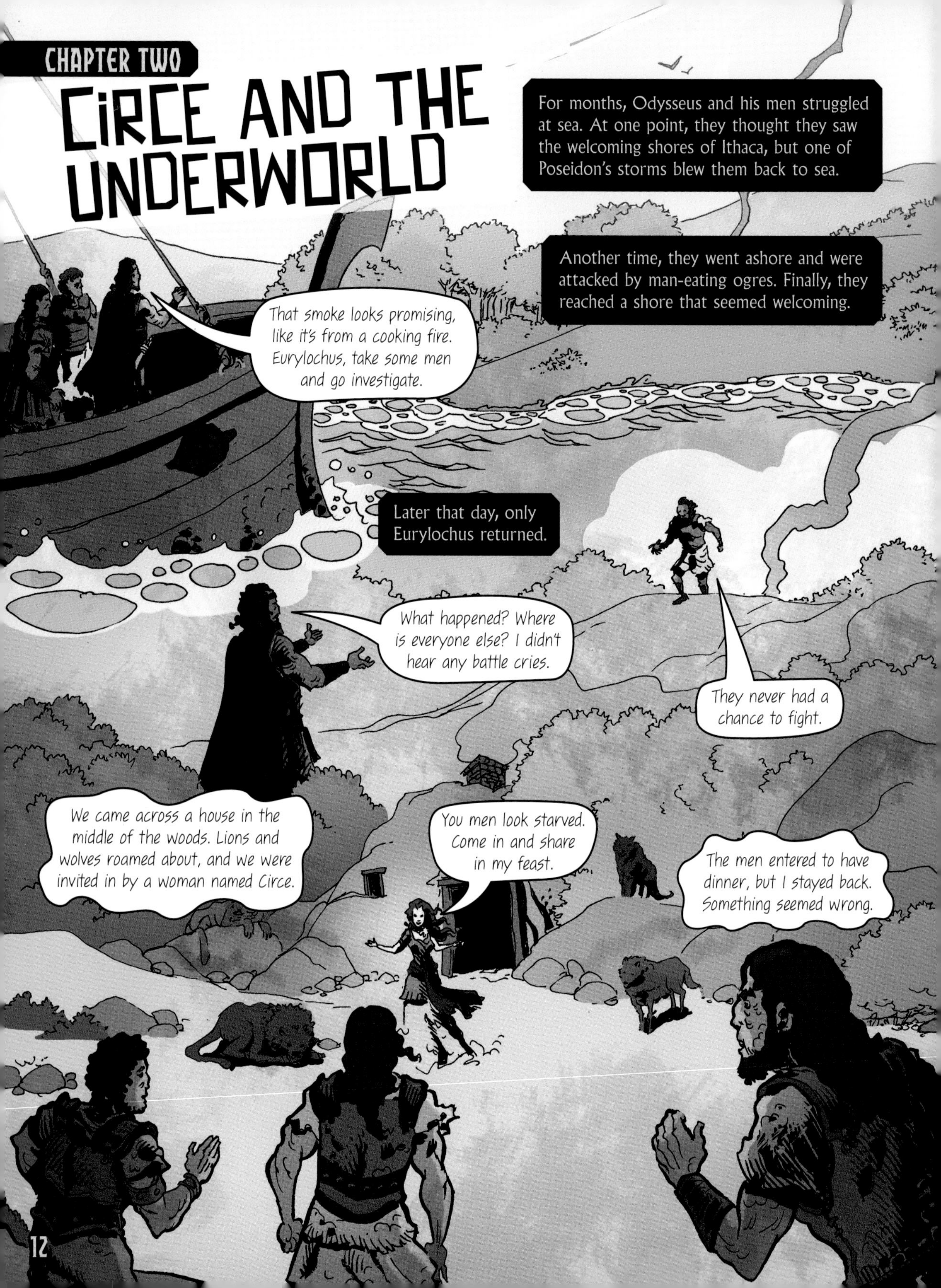
For months, Odysseus and his men struggled at sea. At one point, they thought they saw the welcoming shores of Ithaca, but one of Poseidon's storms blew them back to sea.
Another time, they went ashore and were attacked by man-eating ogres. Finally, they reached a shore that seemed welcoming.
That smoke looks promising, like it's from a cooking fire. Eurylochus, take some men and go investigate.
Later that day, only Eurylochus returned.
What happened? Where is everyone else? I didn't hear any battle cries.
They never had a chance to fight.
We came across a house in the middle of the woods. Lions and wolves roamed about, and we were invited in by a woman named Circe.
You men look starved. Come in and share in my feast.
The men entered to have dinner, but I stayed back. Something seemed wrong.

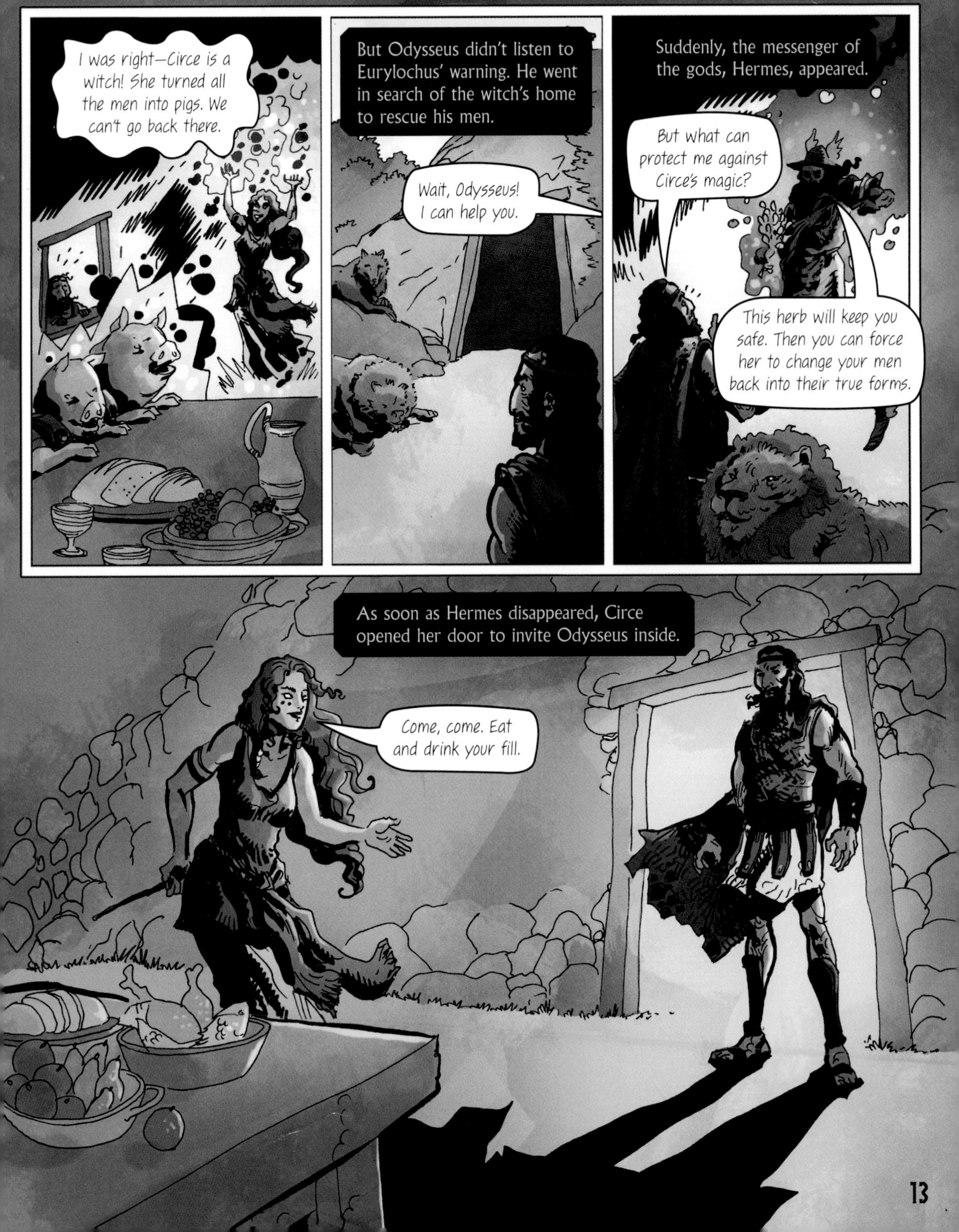
I was right—Circe is a witch! She turned all the men into pigs. We can't go back there.
But Odysseus didn't listen to Eurylochus' warning. He went in search of the witch's home to rescue his men.
Wait, Odysseus! I can help you.
Suddenly, the messenger of the gods, Hermes, appeared.
But what can protect me against Circe's magic?
This herb will keep you safe. Then you can force her to change your men back into their true forms.
As soon as Hermes disappeared, Circe opened her door to invite Odysseus inside.
Come, come. Eat and drink your fill.

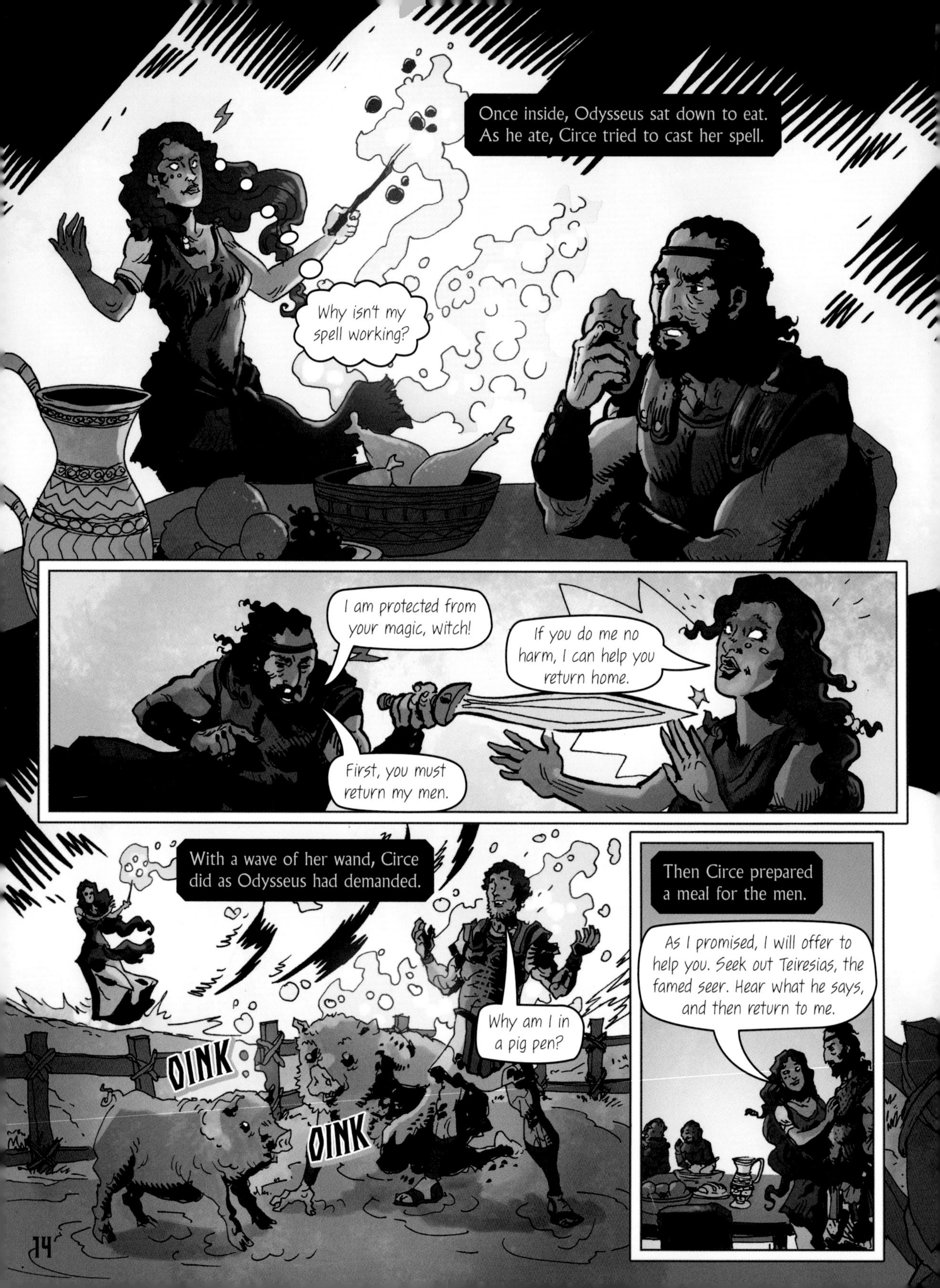

Once inside, Odysseus sat down to eat. As he ate, Circe tried to cast her spell.
Why isn't my spell working?
I am protected from your magic, witch!
First, you must return my men.
If you do me no harm, I can help you return home.
With a wave of her wand, Circe did as Odysseus had demanded.
Why am I in a pig pen?
OINK
OINK
Then Circe prepared a meal for the men.
As I promised, I will offer to help you. Seek out Teiresias, the famed seer. Hear what he says, and then return to me.

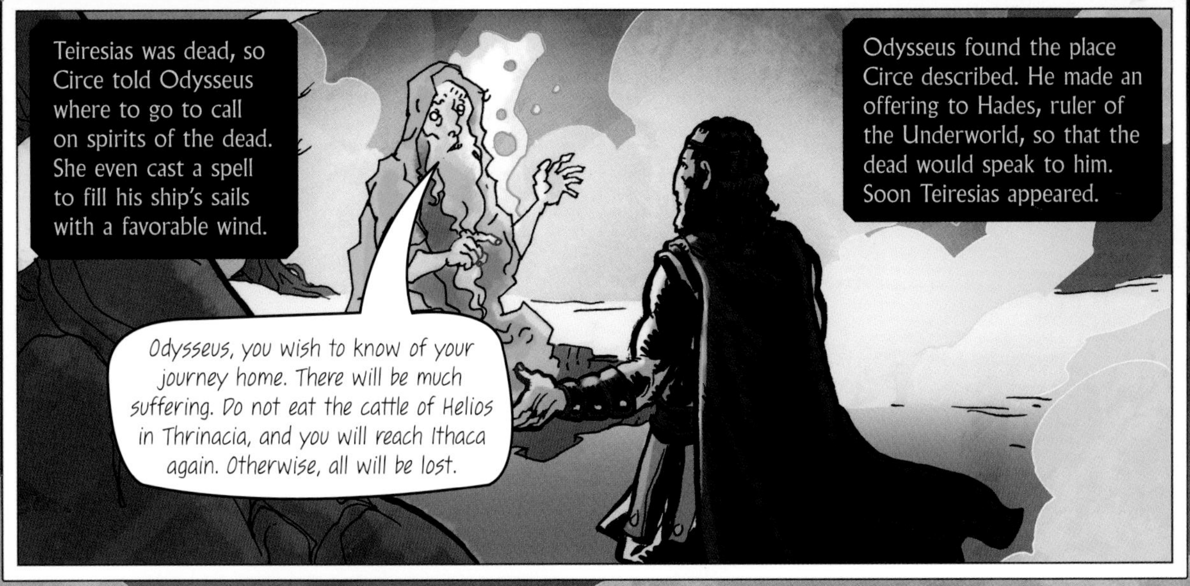
Teiresias was dead, so Circe told Odysseus where to go to call on spirits of the dead. She even cast a spell to fill his ship's sails with a favorable wind.
Odysseus found the place Circe described. He made an offering to Hades, ruler of the Underworld, so that the dead would speak to him. Soon Teiresias appeared.
Odysseus, you wish to know of your journey home. There will be much suffering. Do not eat the cattle of Helios in Thrinacia, and you will reach Ithaca again. Otherwise, all will be lost.

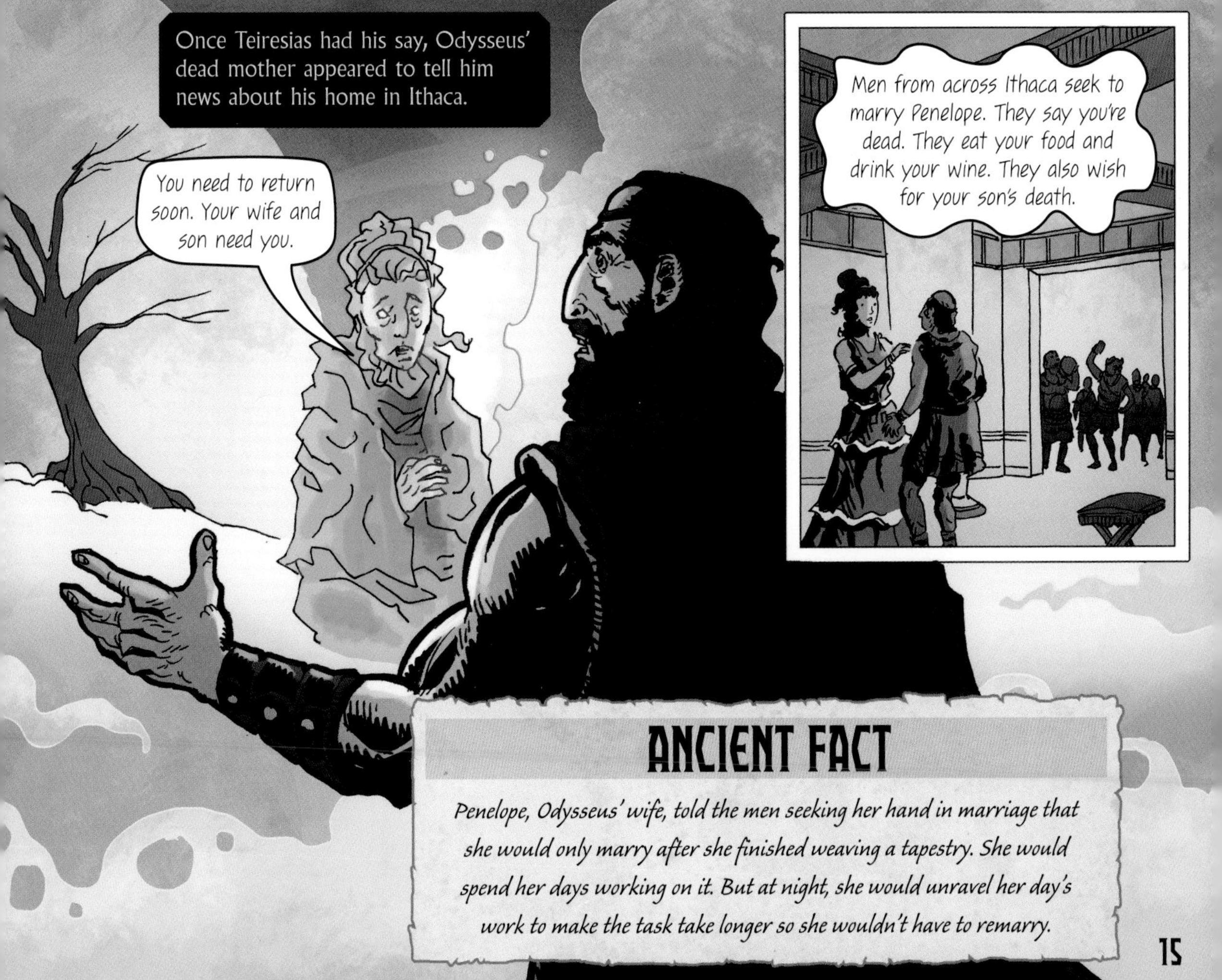
Once Teiresias had his say, Odysseus' dead mother appeared to tell him news about his home in Ithaca.
You need to return soon. Your wife and son need you.
Men from across Ithaca seek to marry Penelope. They say you're dead. They eat your food and drink your wine. They also wish for your son's death.

ANCIENT FACT

Penelope, Odysseus' wife, told the men seeking her hand in marriage that she would only marry after she finished weaving a tapestry. She would spend her days working on it. But at night, she would unravel her day's work to make the task take longer so she wouldn't have to remarry.

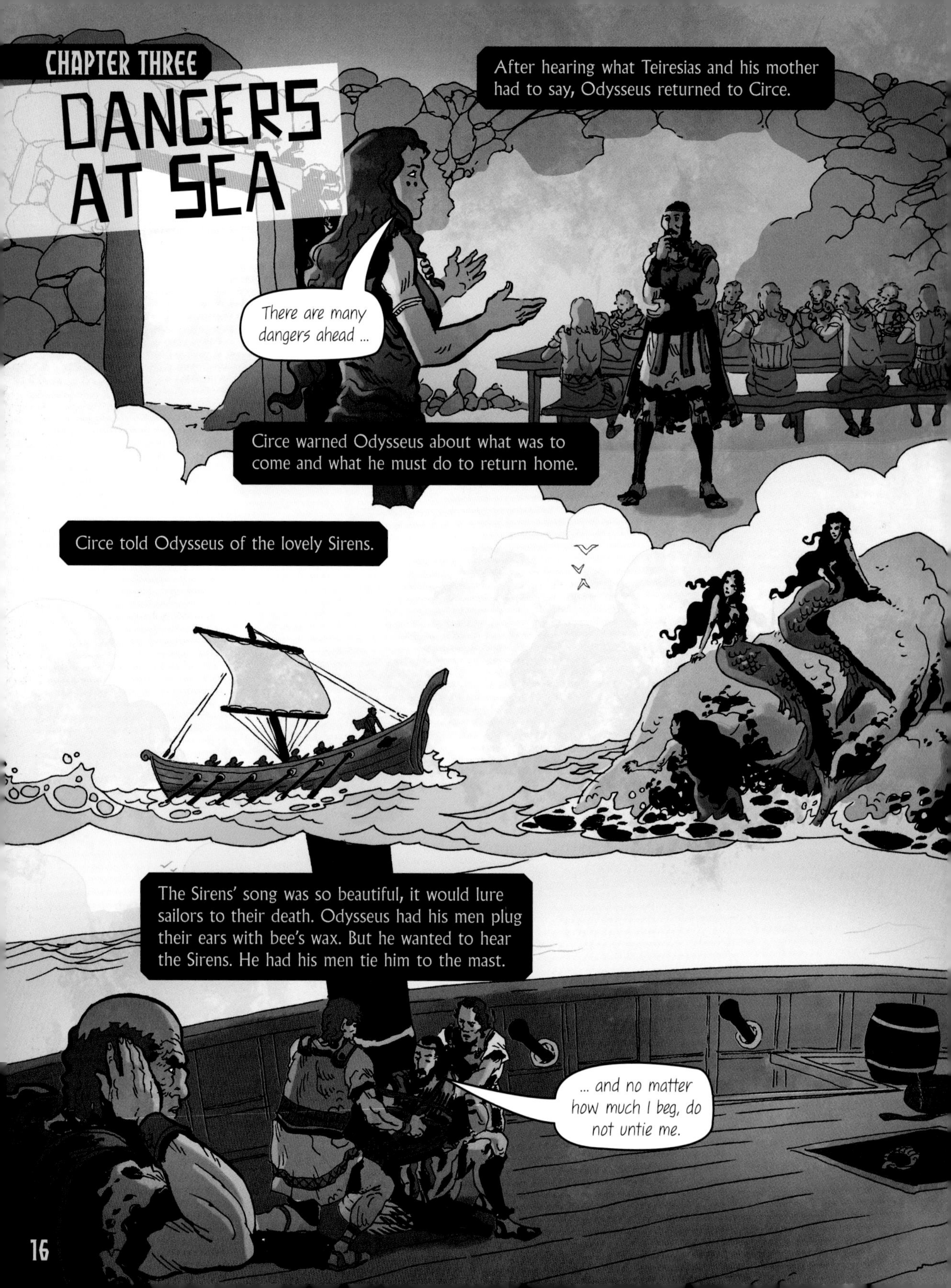
CHAPTER THREE
DANGERS AT SEA
After hearing what Teiresias and his mother had to say, Odysseus returned to Circe.
There are many dangers ahead ...
Circe warned Odysseus about what was to come and what he must do to return home.
Circe told Odysseus of the lovely Sirens.
The Sirens' song was so beautiful, it would lure sailors to their death. Odysseus had his men plug their ears with bee's wax. But he wanted to hear the Sirens. He had his men tie him to the mast.
... and no matter how much I beg, do not untie me.

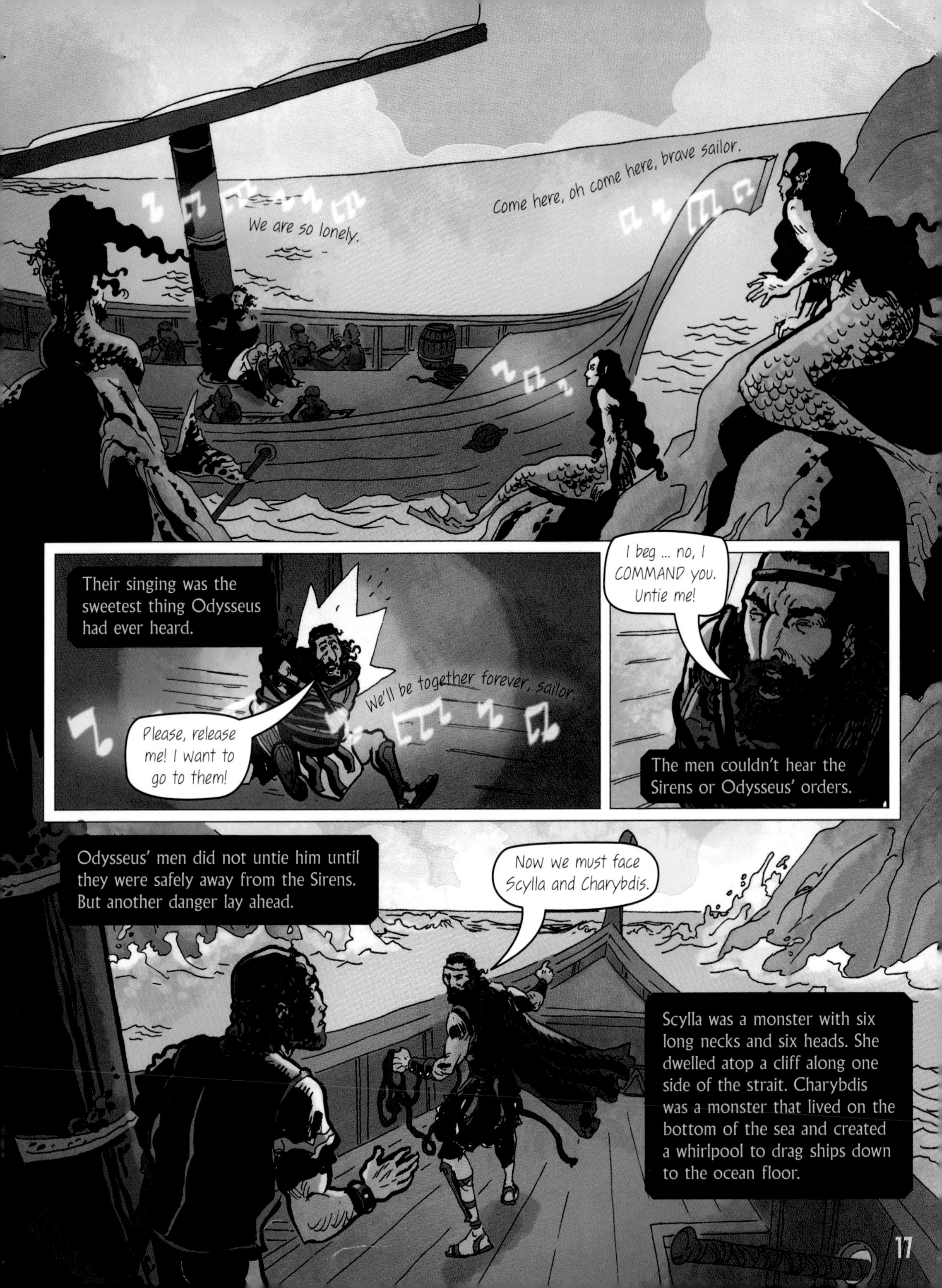
We are so lonely.
Come here, oh come here, brave sailor.
Their singing was the sweetest thing Odysseus had ever heard.
We'll be together forever, sailor.
Please, release me! I want to go to them!
I beg ... no, I COMMAND you. Untie me!
The men couldn't hear the Sirens or Odysseus' orders.
Odysseus' men did not untie him until they were safely away from the Sirens. But another danger lay ahead.
Now we must face Scylla and Charybdis.
Scylla was a monster with six long necks and six heads. She dwelled atop a cliff along one side of the strait. Charybdis was a monster that lived on the bottom of the sea and created a whirlpool to drag ships down to the ocean floor.

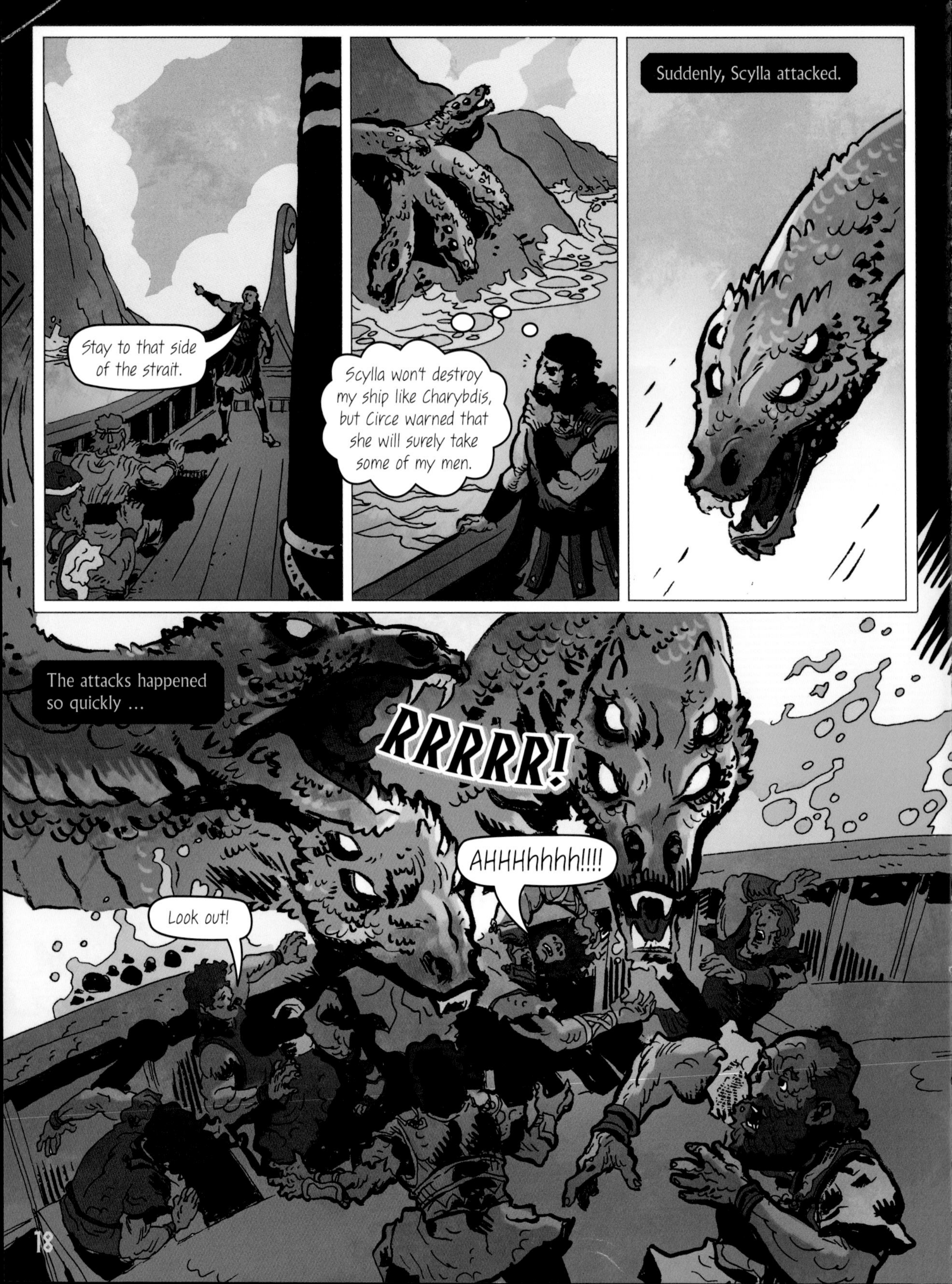
Suddenly, Scylla attacked.
Stay to that side of the strait.
Scylla won't destroy my ship like Charybdis, but Circe warned that she will surely take some of my men.
The attacks happened so quickly ...
RRRRR!
AHHHhhhh!!!!
Look out!

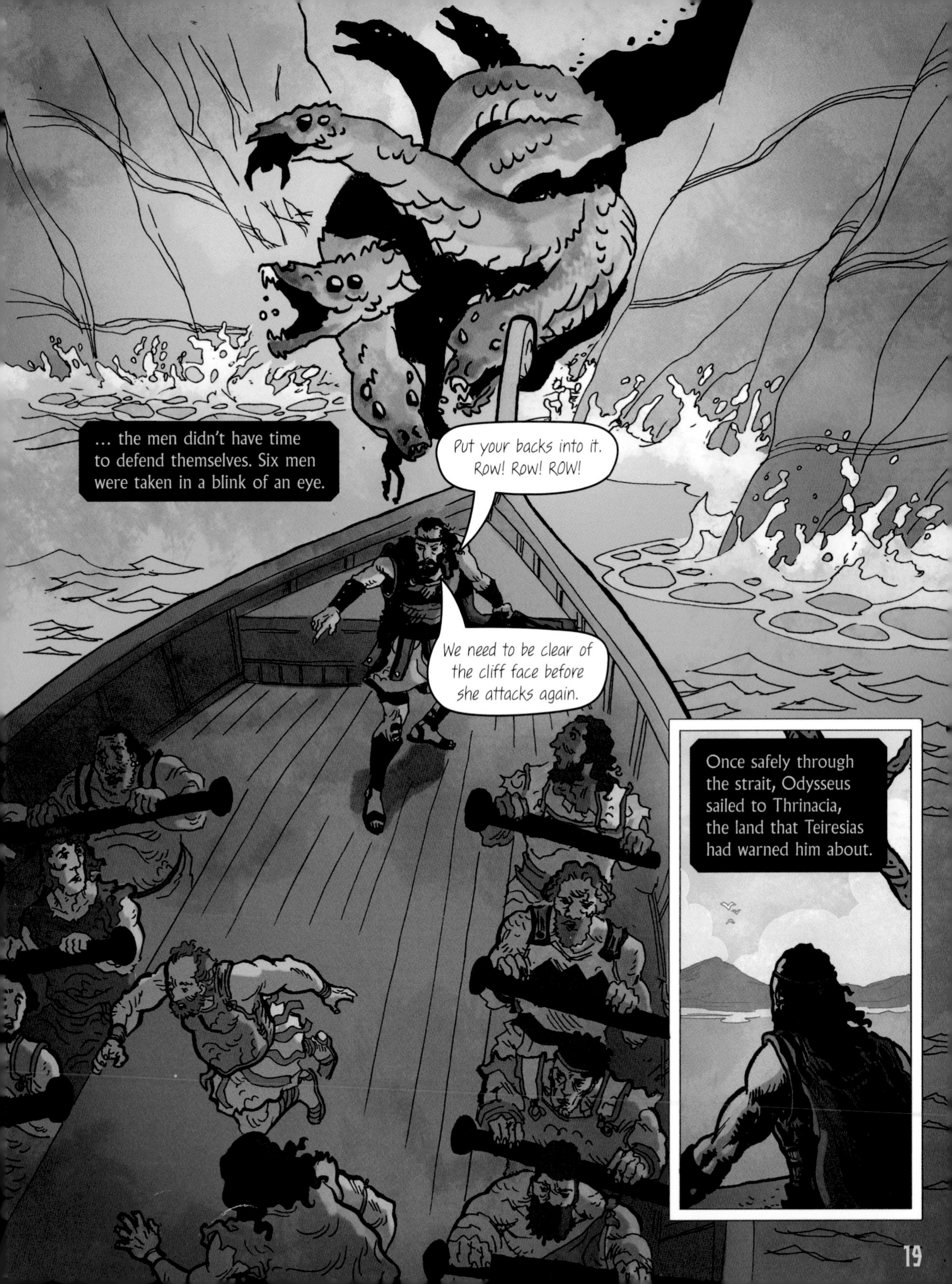
... the men didn't have time to defend themselves. Six men were taken in a blink of an eye.
Put your backs into it. Row! Row! ROW!
We need to be clear of the cliff face before she attacks again.
Once safely through the strait, Odysseus sailed to Thrinacia, the land that Teiresias had warned him about.

CHAPTER FOUR

SHIPWRECKED

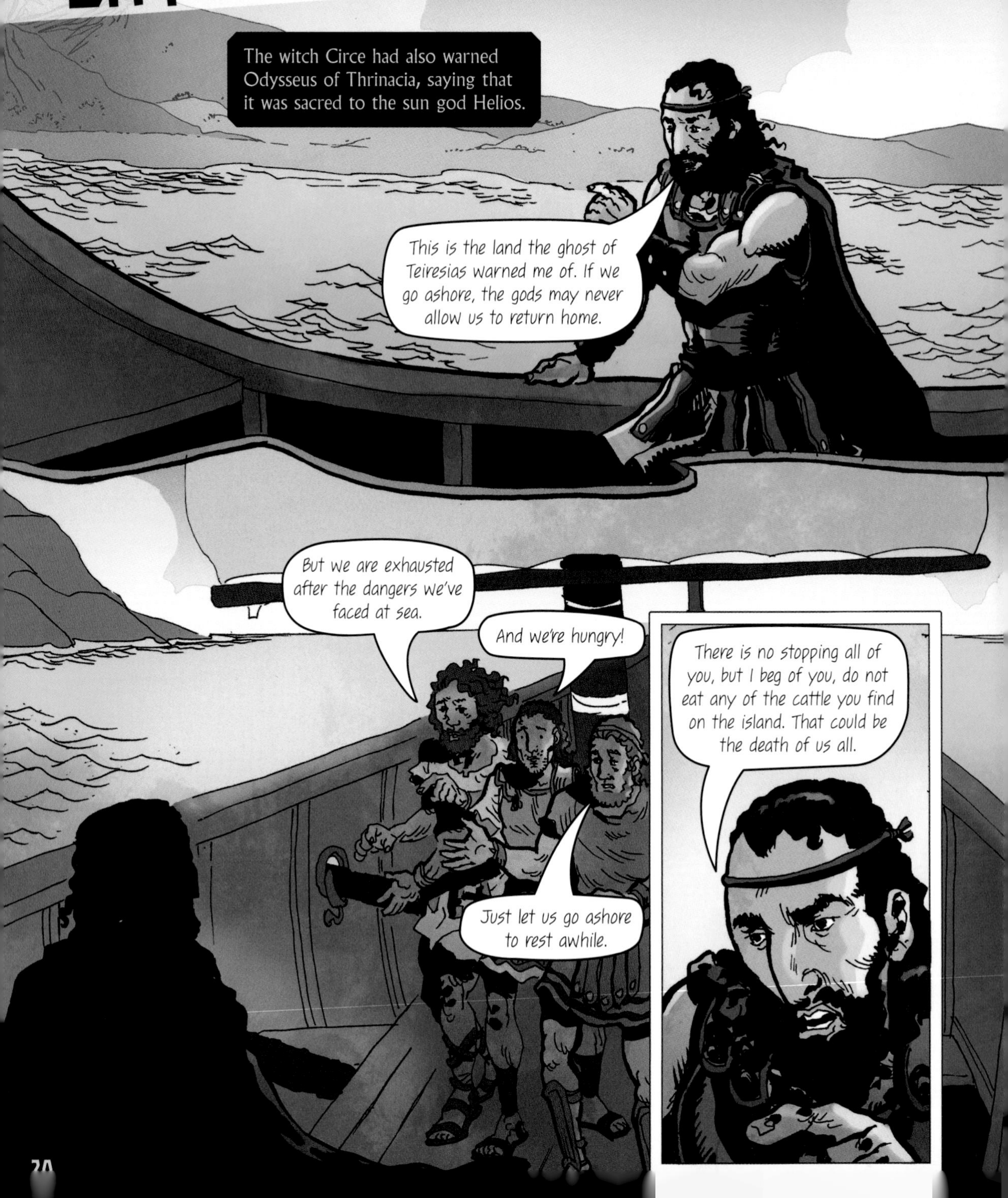

The witch Circe had also warned Odysseus of Thrinacia, saying that it was sacred to the sun god Helios.
This is the land the ghost of Teiresias warned me of. If we go ashore, the gods may never allow us to return home.
But we are exhausted after the dangers we've faced at sea.
And we're hungry!
Just let us go ashore to rest awhile.
There is no stopping all of you, but I beg of you, do not eat any of the cattle you find on the island. That could be the death of us all.

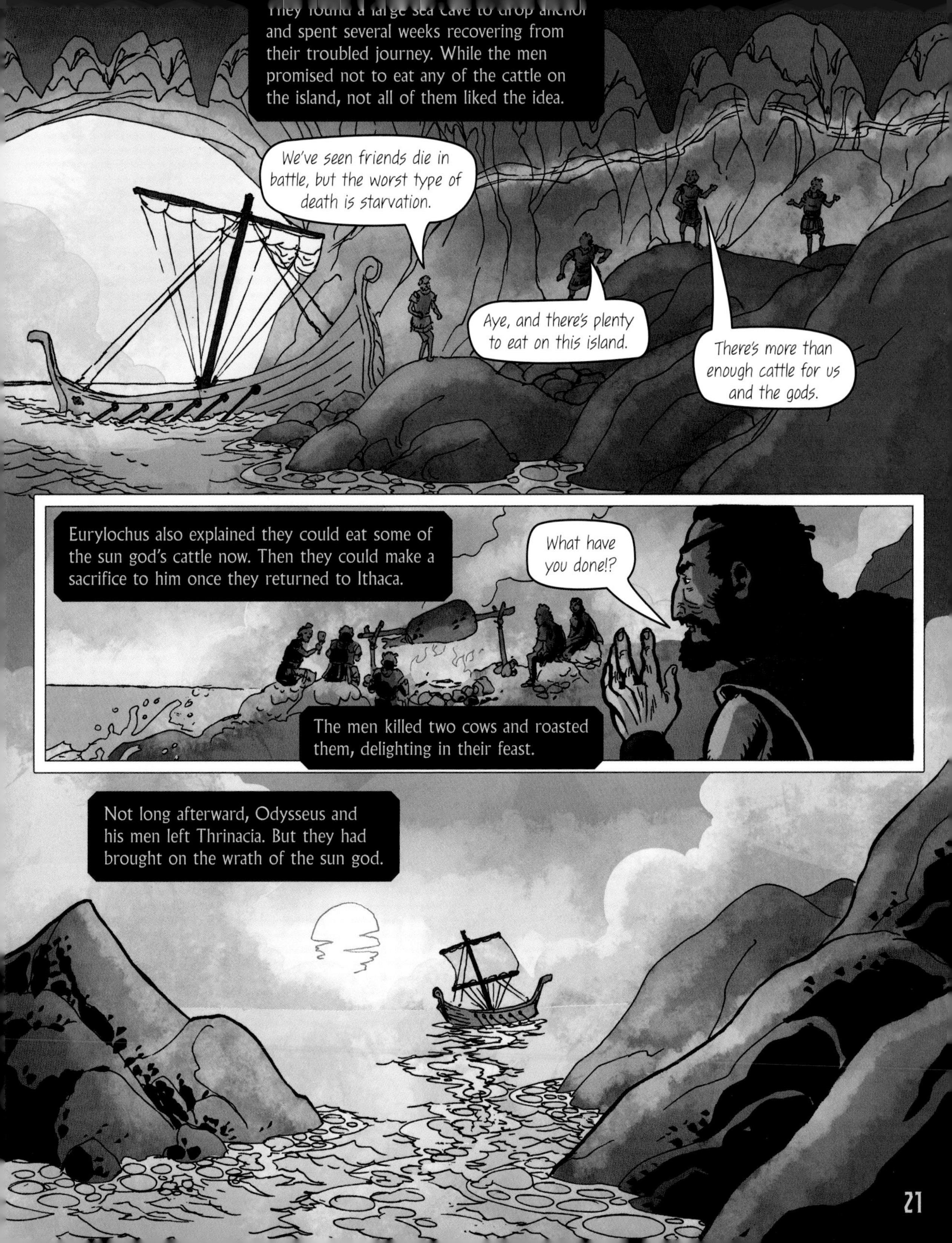
They found a large sea cave to drop anchor and spent several weeks recovering from their troubled journey. While the men promised not to eat any of the cattle on the island, not all of them liked the idea.
We've seen friends die in battle, but the worst type of death is starvation.
Aye, and there's plenty to eat on this island.
There's more than enough cattle for us and the gods.
Eurylochus also explained they could eat some of the sun god's cattle now. Then they could make a sacrifice to him once they returned to Ithaca.
What have you done!?
The men killed two cows and roasted them, delighting in their feast.
Not long afterward, Odysseus and his men left Thrinacia. But they had brought on the wrath of the sun god.

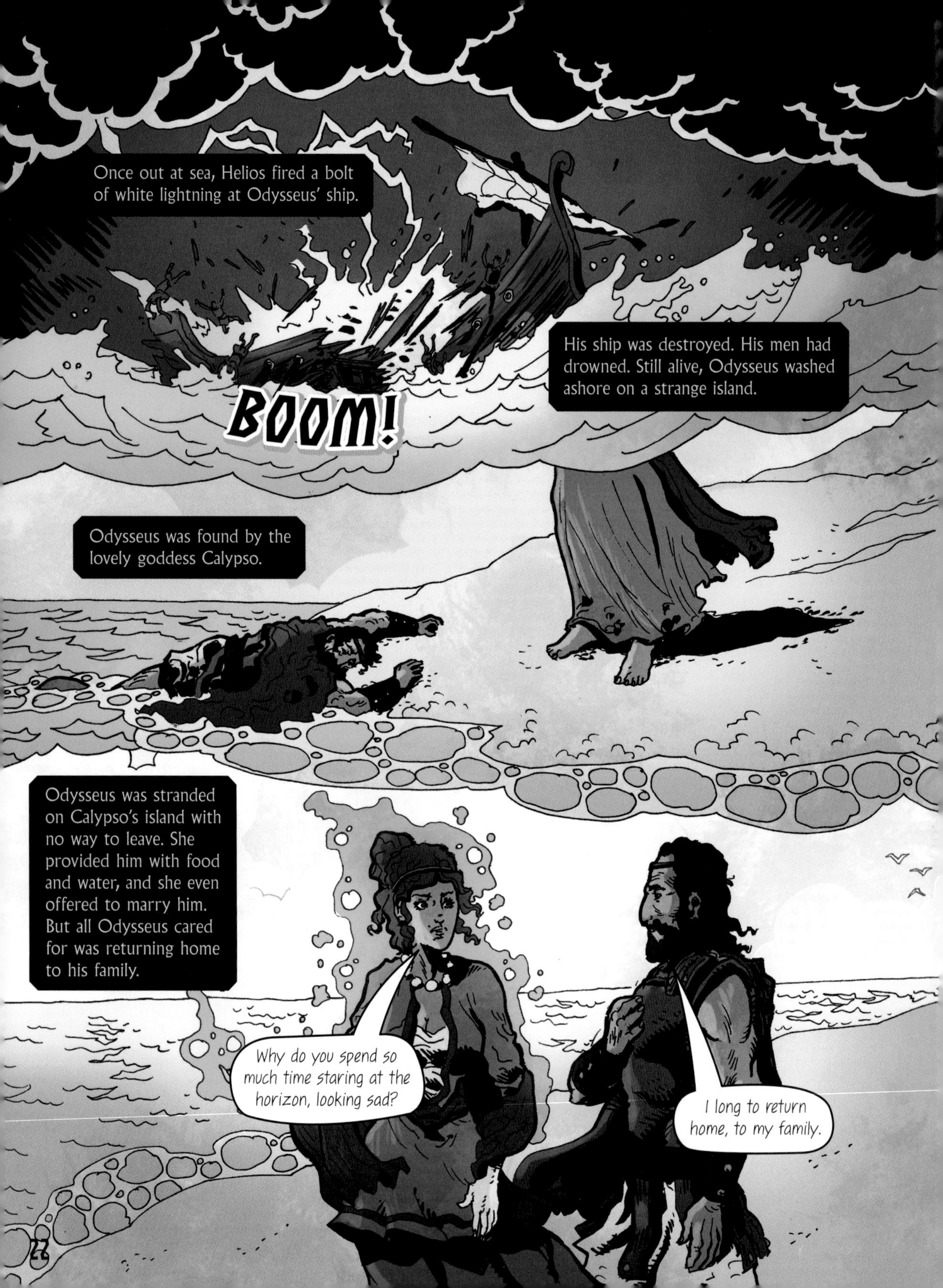

Once out at sea, Helios fired a bolt of white lightning at Odysseus' ship.
BOOM!
His ship was destroyed. His men had drowned. Still alive, Odysseus washed ashore on a strange island.
Odysseus was found by the lovely goddess Calypso.
Odysseus was stranded on Calypso's island with no way to leave. She provided him with food and water, and she even offered to marry him. But all Odysseus cared for was returning home to his family.
Why do you spend so much time staring at the horizon, looking sad?
I long to return home, to my family.

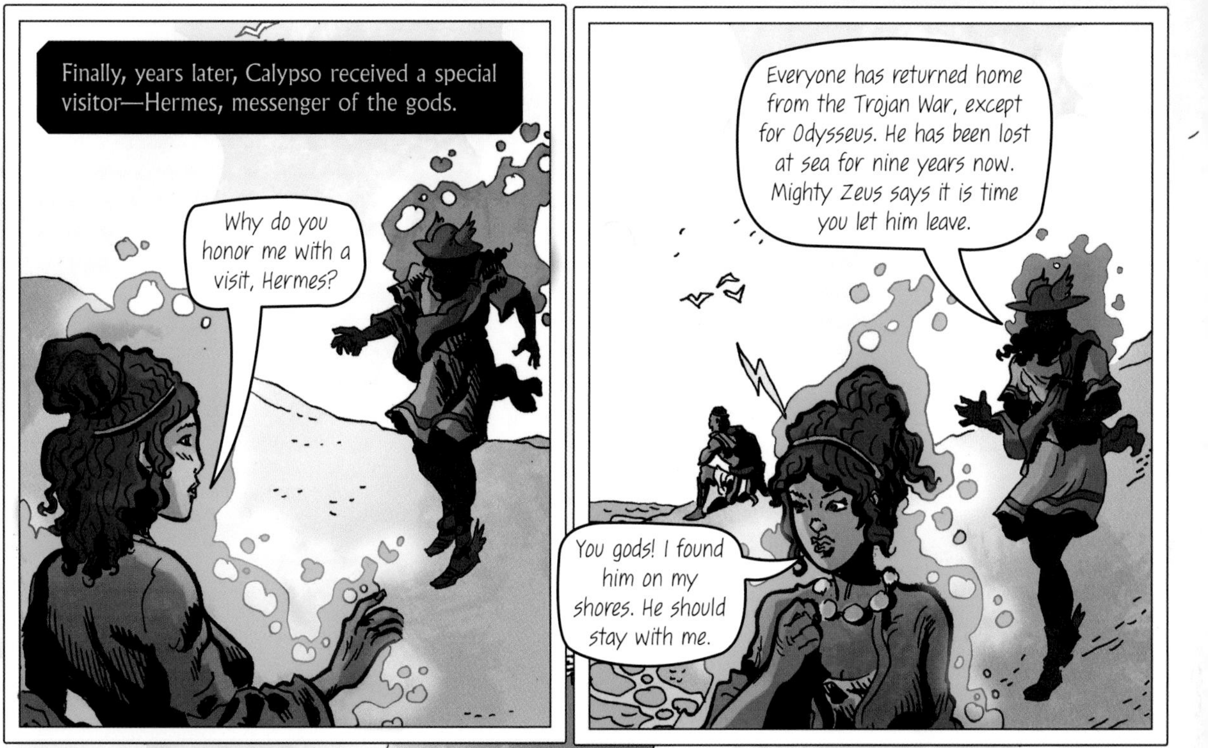
Finally, years later, Calypso received a special visitor—Hermes, messenger of the gods.
Why do you honor me with a visit, Hermes?
Everyone has returned home from the Trojan War, except for Odysseus. He has been lost at sea for nine years now. Mighty Zeus says it is time you let him leave.
You gods! I found him on my shores. He should stay with me.

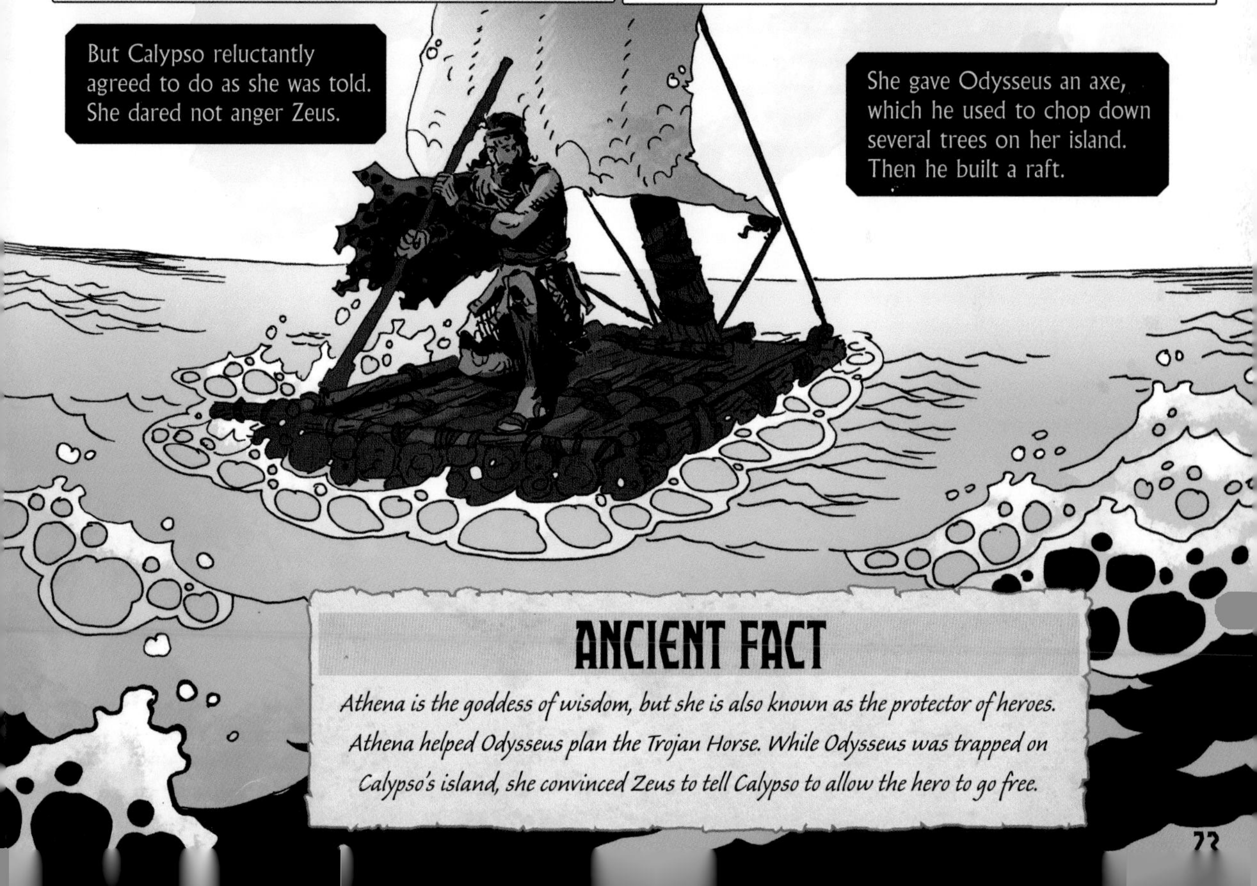
But Calypso reluctantly agreed to do as she was told. She dared not anger Zeus.
She gave Odysseus an axe, which he used to chop down several trees on her island. Then he built a raft.

ANCIENT FACT

Athena is the goddess of wisdom, but she is also known as the protector of heroes. Athena helped Odysseus plan the Trojan Horse. While Odysseus was trapped on Calypso's island, she convinced Zeus to tell Calypso to allow the hero to go free.

HOME, FINALLY

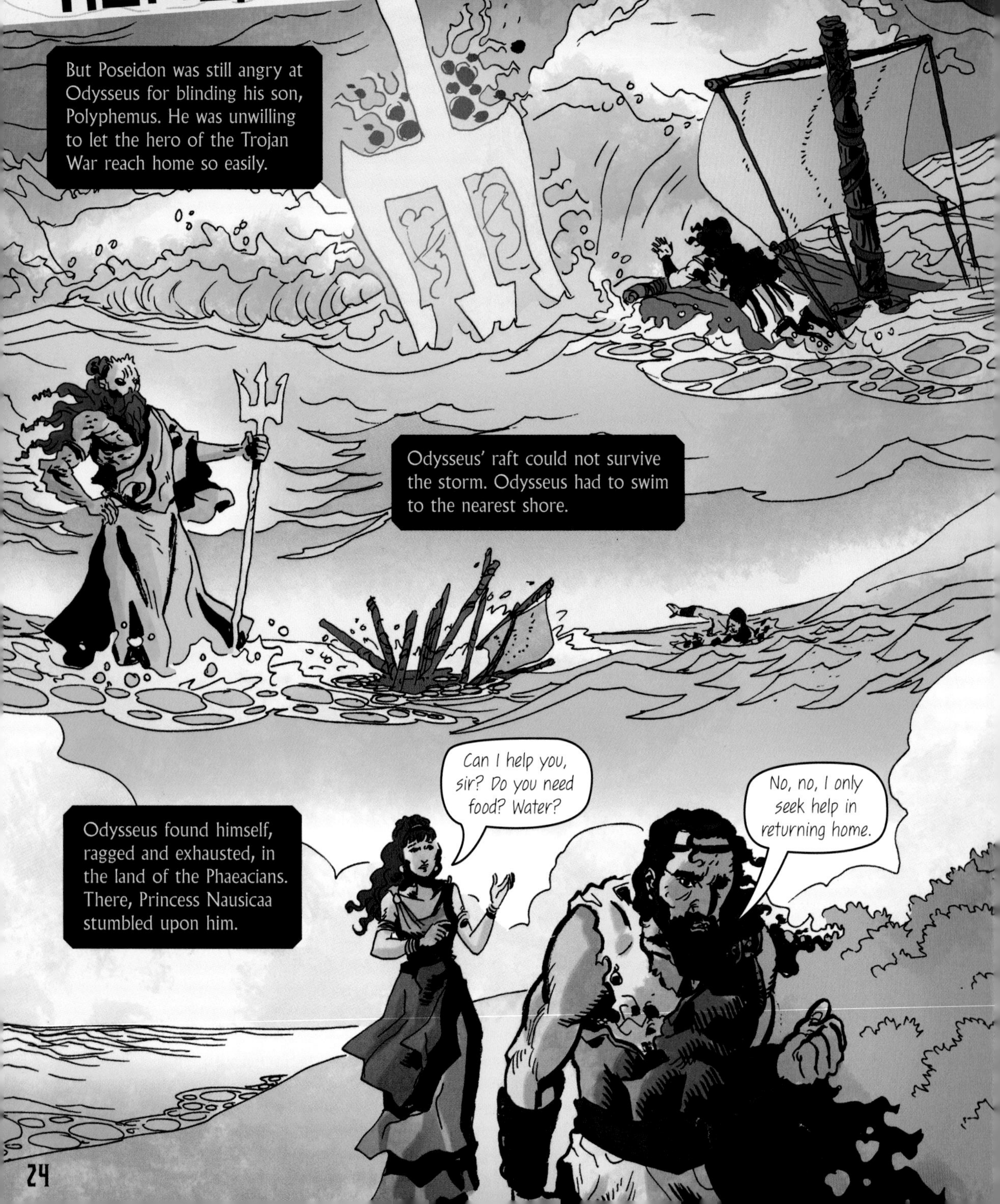

But Poseidon was still angry at Odysseus for blinding his son, Polyphemus. He was unwilling to let the hero of the Trojan War reach home so easily.
Odysseus' raft could not survive the storm. Odysseus had to swim to the nearest shore.
Odysseus found himself, ragged and exhausted, in the land of the Phaeacians. There, Princess Nausicaa stumbled upon him.
Can I help you, sir? Do you need food? Water?
No, no, I only seek help in returning home.

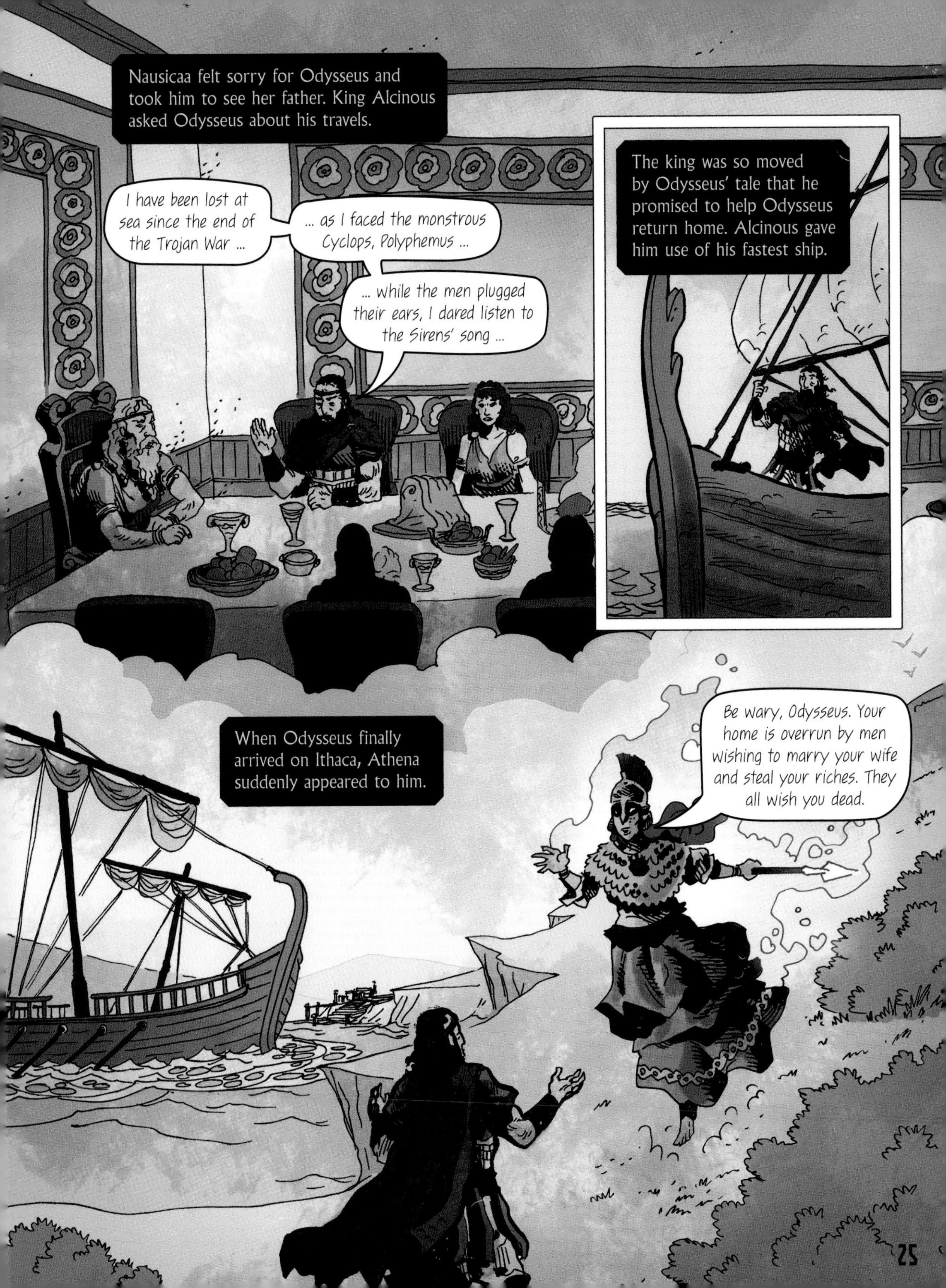

Nausicaa felt sorry for Odysseus and took him to see her father. King Alcinous asked Odysseus about his travels.
I have been lost at sea since the end of the Trojan War ...
... as I faced the monstrous Cyclops, Polyphemus ...
... while the men plugged their ears, I dared listen to the Sirens' song ...
The king was so moved by Odysseus' tale that he promised to help Odysseus return home. Alcinous gave him use of his fastest ship.
When Odysseus finally arrived on Ithaca, Athena suddenly appeared to him.
Be wary, Odysseus. Your home is overrun by men wishing to marry your wife and steal your riches. They all wish you dead.

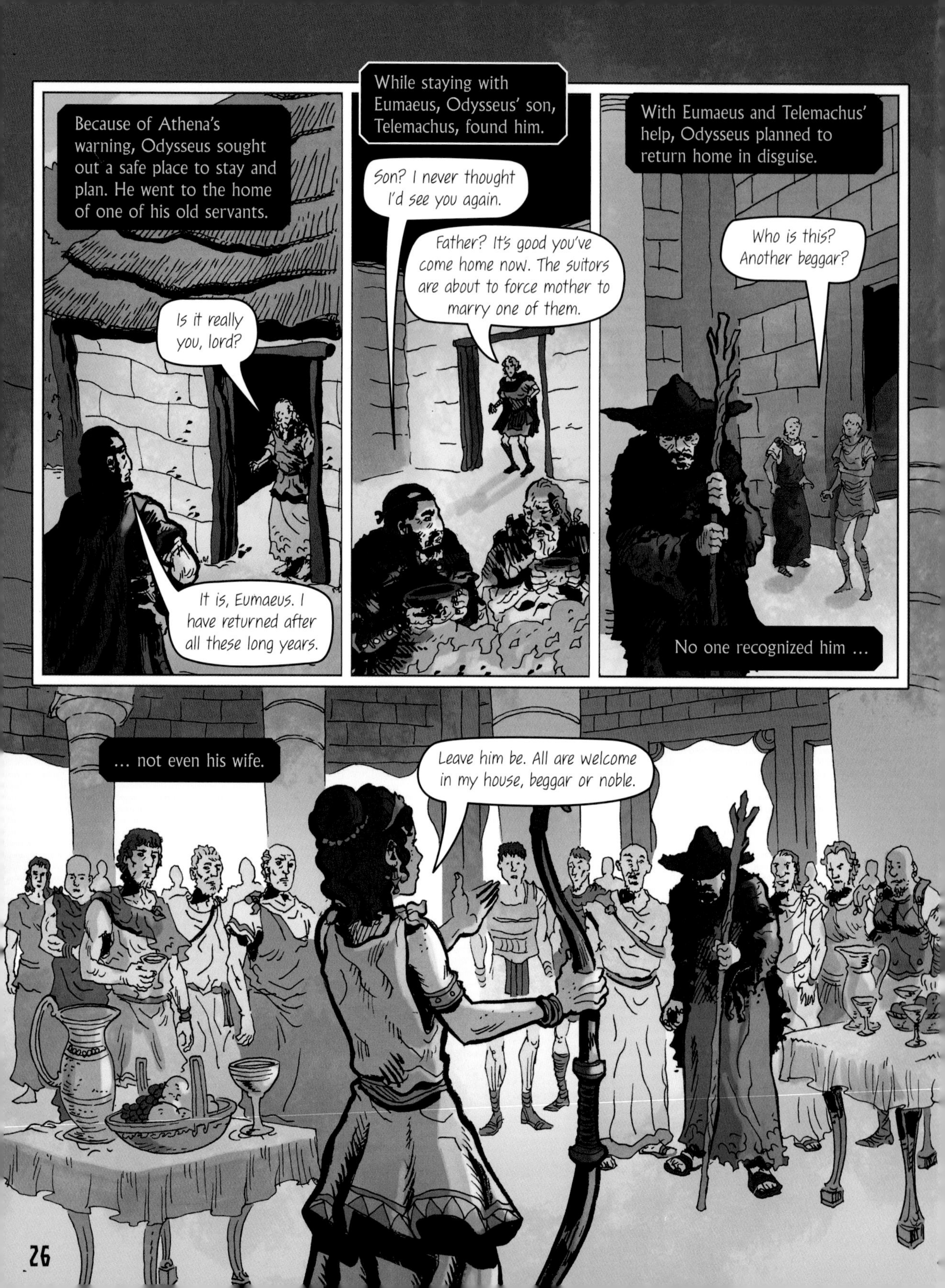
Because of Athena's warning, Odysseus sought out a safe place to stay and plan. He went to the home of one of his old servants.
Is it really you, lord?
It is, Eumaeus. I have returned after all these long years.
While staying with Eumaeus, Odysseus' son, Telemachus, found him.
Son? I never thought I'd see you again.
Father? It's good you've come home now. The suitors are about to force mother to marry one of them.
With Eumaeus and Telemachus' help, Odysseus planned to return home in disguise.
Who is this? Another beggar?
No one recognized him ...
... not even his wife.
Leave him be. All are welcome in my house, beggar or noble.

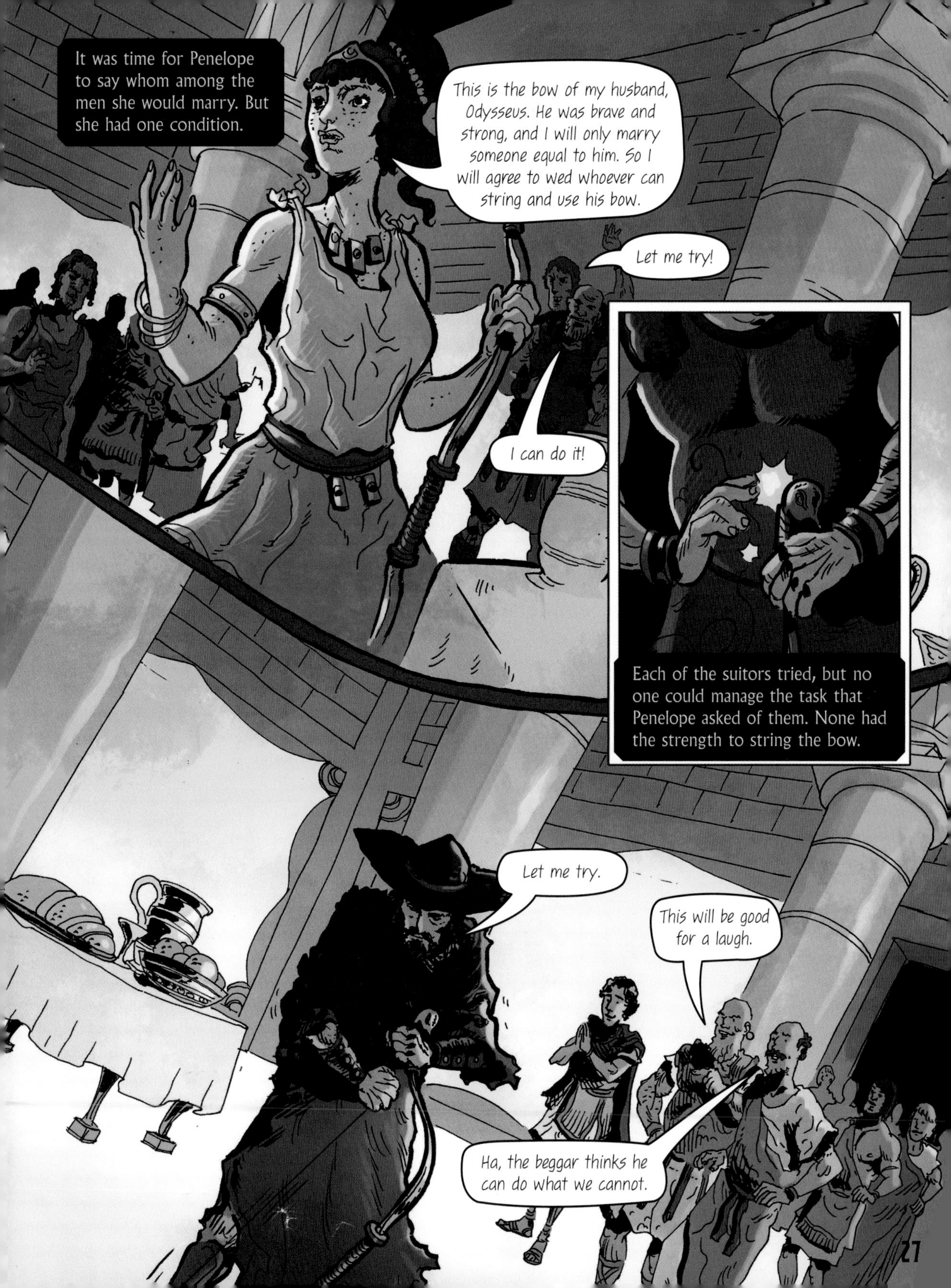
It was time for Penelope to say whom among the men she would marry. But she had one condition.
This is the bow of my husband, Odysseus. He was brave and strong, and I will only marry someone equal to him. So I will agree to wed whoever can string and use his bow.
Let me try!
I can do it!
Each of the suitors tried, but no one could manage the task that Penelope asked of them. None had the strength to string the bow.
Let me try.
This will be good for a laugh.
Ha, the beggar thinks he can do what we cannot.

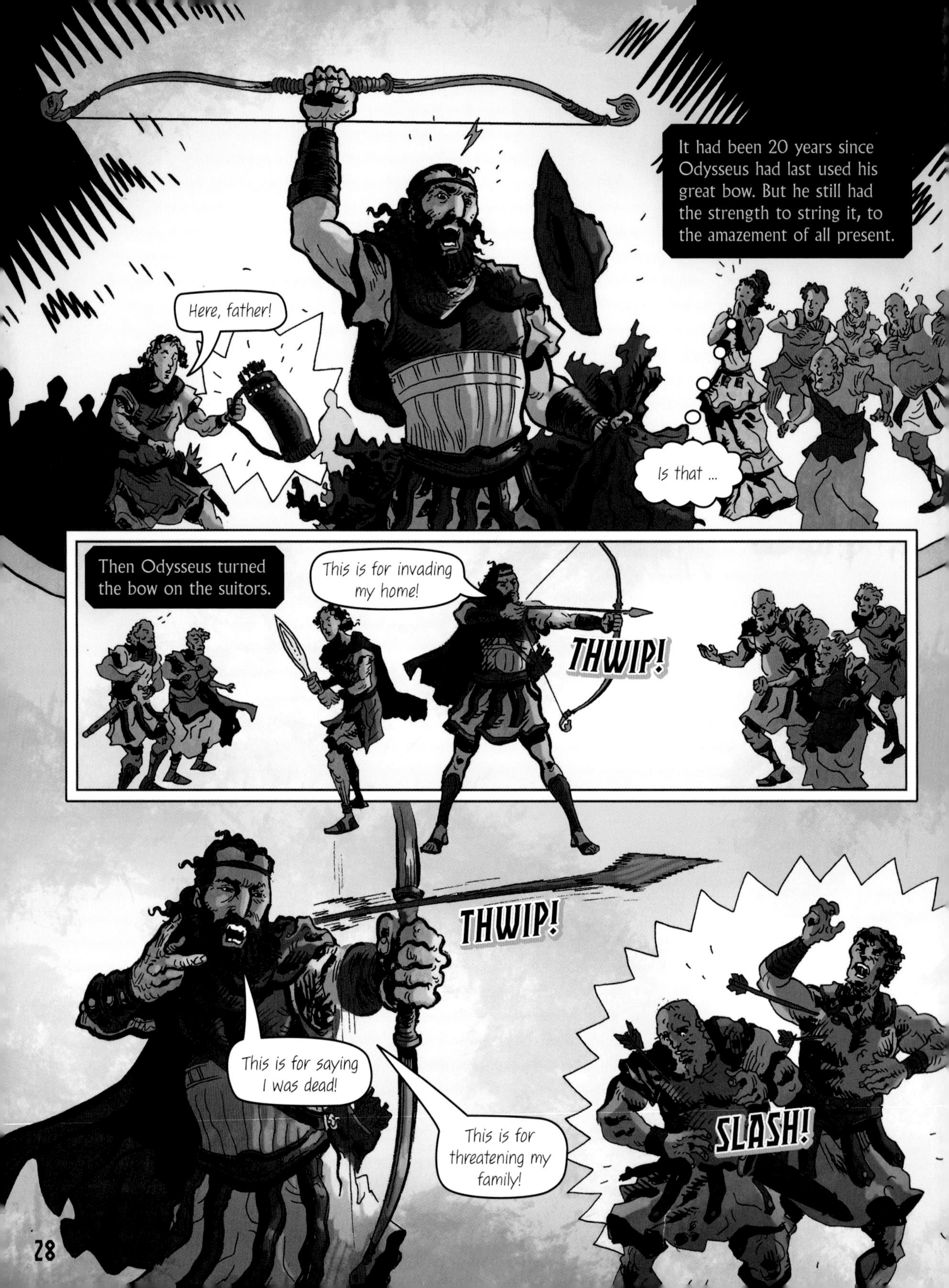
It had been 20 years since Odysseus had last used his great bow. But he still had the strength to string it, to the amazement of all present.
Here, father!
Is that ...
Then Odysseus turned the bow on the suitors.
This is for invading my home!
THWIP!
THWIP!
This is for saying I was dead!
This is for threatening my family!
SLASH!

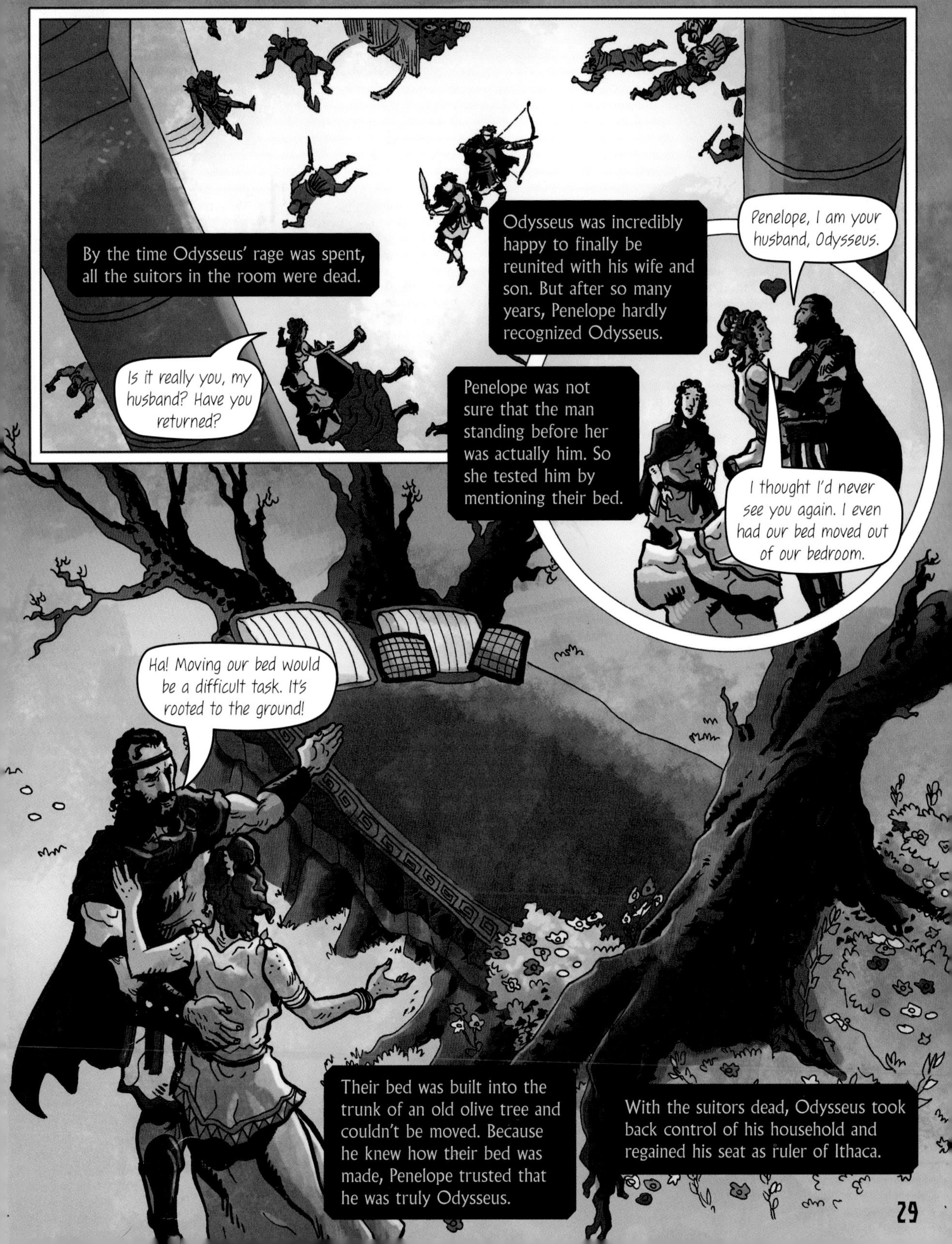
By the time Odysseus' rage was spent, all the suitors in the room were dead.
Is it really you, my husband? Have you returned?
Odysseus was incredibly happy to finally be reunited with his wife and son. But after so many years, Penelope hardly recognized Odysseus.
Penelope, I am your husband, Odysseus.
Penelope was not sure that the man standing before her was actually him. So she tested him by mentioning their bed.
I thought I'd never see you again. I even had our bed moved out of our bedroom.
Ha! Moving our bed would be a difficult task. It's rooted to the ground!
Their bed was built into the trunk of an old olive tree and couldn't be moved. Because he knew how their bed was made, Penelope trusted that he was truly Odysseus.
With the suitors dead, Odysseus took back control of his household and regained his seat as ruler of Ithaca.

GLOSSARY

Cyclops (SEYE-klahps)—a one-eyed giant from myths

sacred (SAY-krid)—an important religious item

sacrifice (SAK-ruh-feyss)—something offered to the gods as a way of honoring them

seer (SEE-ur)—a person who has the ability to see the future

strait (STRAYT)—a narrow passage of water that connects two large bodies of water

suitor (SOO-tur)—a man who is trying to persuade a woman to marry him

tapestry (TAP-his-tree)—a thick weaving, often with pictures that is used as a wall hanging

Trojan Horse (TROH-jan HORSS)—a hollow wooden horse that allowed Greek soldiers to sneak into the city of Troy; today it means a person or thing that secretly works to undermine an opponent

Underworld (UN-dur-wurld)—the land of the dead in myths

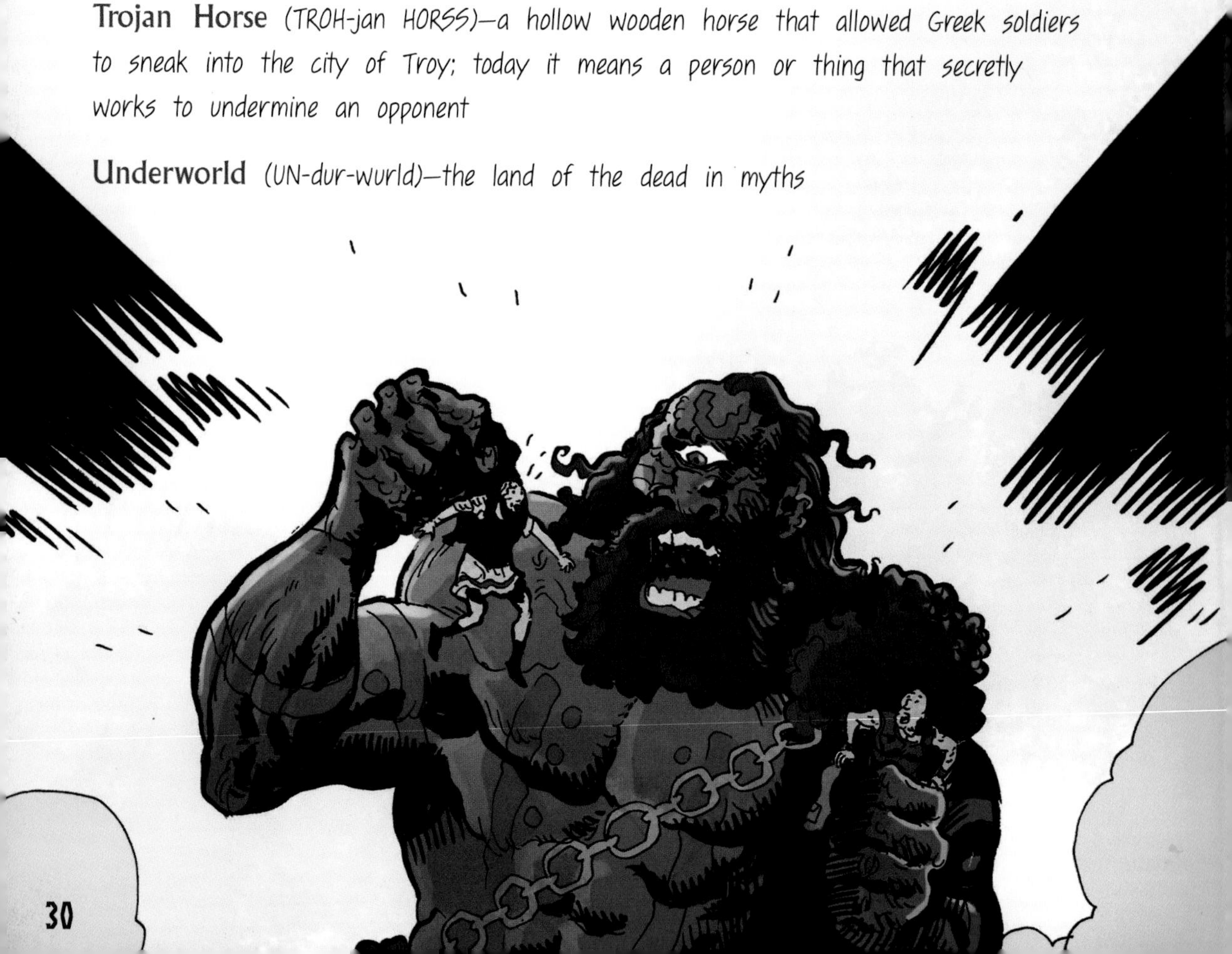

READ MORE

Hoena, Blake. *Everything Mythology*. National Geographic Kids. Washington, D.C.: National Geographic Children's Books, 2014.

Jeffrey, Gary. *Odysseus and the Odyssey*. Graphic Mythical Heroes. New York: Gareth Stevens Pub., 2013.

Olmstead, Kathleen. *The Iliad*. Classic Starts. New York: Sterling Publishing Co., Inc., 2014.

INTERNET SITES

FactHound offers a safe, fun way to find Internet sites related to this book. All of the sites on FactHound have been researched by our staff.

Here's all you do:

Visit *www.facthound.com*

Type in this code: 9781491420768

Super-cool stuff!

Check out projects, games and lots more at
www.capstonekids.com

INDEX

TITLES IN THIS SET

A GRAPHIC RETELLING
THE 12 LABORS OF
HERCULES

A GRAPHIC RETELLING
JASON
AND THE ARGONAUTS

A GRAPHIC RETELLING
THE VOYAGE OF
ODYSSEUS

A GRAPHIC RETELLING
THE
ADVENTURES OF
PERSEUS

A GRAPHIC RETELLING
THESEUS
AND THE MINOTAUR

A GRAPHIC RETELLING
THE
TROJAN WAR

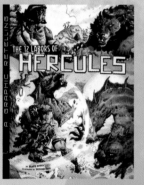

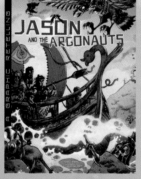

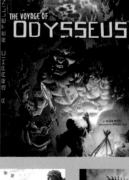

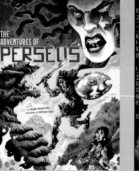

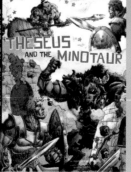

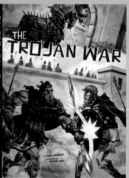